ANTI-SEMITISM
The Jewish Response

Derek J. Penslar

BEHRMAN HOUSE

CONTENTS

FOR JOSHUA

D.P.

COVER DESIGN: ROBERT J. O'DELL
TYPESETTING AND BOOK DESIGN: MULTIFACIT GRAPHICS INC.
PROJECT EDITOR: ADAM SIEGEL

© COPYRIGHT 1989 BY BEHRMAN HOUSE, INC.
235 WATCHUNG AVENUE, WEST ORANGE, NEW JERSEY 07502
ISBN 0-87441-494-6
MANUFACTURED IN THE UNITED STATES OF AMERICA

PREFACE

The French philosopher Jean-Paul Sartre once wrote, "The Jews have neither community of interests nor community of beliefs. They do not have the same fatherland; they have no history. The sole tie that binds them is the hostility and disdain of the societies which surround them . . ."

That is, Sartre believed that people are aware of something called Jewishness only because they are hated for it. "It is the anti-Semite," and only the anti-Semite, "who creates the Jew."*

What historical facts or events could have led Sartre to write these famous lines? Clearly, the Jewish spirit depends on neither love nor hatred from non-Jews for its survival. The fact remains, however, that anti-Semitism has been a powerful force in the shaping of Jewish history. Not only has it physically touched the lives of many Jews, it has profoundly influenced their thinking as well.

Jewish responses to anti-Semitism have been varied and complex. Anti-Semitism has led Jews to strengthen their commitment to their faith and communities. At times, however, Jews confronted with anti-Semitism have escaped from their faith and people in order to be accepted by the non-Jewish world. This book provides a sampling of these and other responses to anti-Semitism throughout Jewish history. For the most part, the book lets the Jews and their opponents speak for themselves—dozens of documents covering two thousand years have been included. The commentary provides historical background and some suggested interpretations.

Any work on Jewish-gentile relations confronts a number of sensitive issues. One must strive to avoid the all-too-common view that Jewish history has been one of ceaseless persecution. It is important to discern shades and varieties within the general phenomenon called "anti-Semitism." History must emerge as the story of real people, subtle and complex, not cardboard cutouts marching across a black-and-white background. It is the author's hope that this book meets at least some of these conditions.

* Sartre, Jean-Paul. *Anti-Semite and Jew*. New York: Schocken, 1948, pp. 91, 143.

3

Antiochus Epiphanes, whose profile is featured on this Greek coin from the second century, was one of the most tyrannical rulers the Jewish people ever had to endure. His insistence that anyone who observed the Jewish religion should be put to death incited the Jews, under the leadership of Judah Maccabee, to a triumphant revolt.

THE ANCIENT WORLD

The Book of Maccabees is known to us as the principal source of the story of Hanukkah. What most of us don't realize, however, is that this story probably recounts the first struggle for religious freedom in man's history. As children we are taught that wicked King Antiochus unleashed a war against Judaism, triggering a heroic Jewish revolt led by Judah Maccabee. Naturally enough, when we celebrate Hanukkah, we focus on the glorious aspects of the story—the Jews' military victory over the Syrian Greeks and the rededication of the Temple—rather than the circumstances that led up to the Maccabean revolt. But a hard look at the people against whom Judah Maccabee fought reveals some of the basic attitudes and beliefs which have often led to anti-Semitism as well as some of the ways the Jews have chosen to respond to such threats.

In 175 B.C.E., Antiochus Epiphanes became king of Syria, which ruled Judea.

It was then that there emerged from Israel a set of renegades who led many people astray. "Come," they said, "let us reach an understanding with the pagans surrounding us, for since we separated ourselves from them many misfortunes have overtaken us." This proposal proved acceptable, and a number of the people eagerly approached the king, who authorized them to practice the pagan observances. So they built a gymnasium in Jerusalem, such as the pagans have, disguised their circumcision, and abandoned the holy covenant, submitting to the heathen rule as willing slaves of impiety....

Then the king issued a proclamation to his whole kingdom that all were to become one single people, each renouncing his particular customs. All the pagans conformed to the king's decree, and many Israelites chose to accept his religion, sacrificing to idols and profaning the sabbath. The king also sent instructions by messenger to Jerusalem and the towns of Judah directing them to adopt customs foreign to the country, banning burnt-offerings, sacrifices and libations from the sanctuary, profaning sabbaths and feasts, defiling the sanctuary and the sacred ministers, building altars, precincts and shrines for idols, sacrificing pigs and unclean beasts, leaving their sons uncircumcized, and prostituting themselves to all kinds of impurity and abomination, so that they should forget the Law and revoke all observance of it....

Many of the people—that is, every apostate from the Law—rallied to [the king's decrees], and so committed evil in the country, forcing Israel into hiding in all their places of refuge. On the fifteenth day of Kislev in the year 145 (December 8, 167 B.C.E.), the abomination [a statue of Olympian Zeus] was erected above the altar [of the Temple] and on the 25th of Kislev they offered sacrifices on the altar....Any books of the Torah that came to light were torn up and burned. Whenever anyone was discovered possessing a copy of the covenant or practicing the Law, the king's decree sentenced him to death ....

Yet there were many in Israel who stood firm and found the courage to refuse unclean food. They chose death rather than contamination by such fare or profanation of the holy covenant, and they were executed. It was a dreadful wrath that visited Israel [1 Maccabees 1].

The clash of religious ideologies and religious restrictions placed upon the Jews as described in the Book of Maccabees reveals a tension between Jews and non-Jews that has existed since ancient times. It is a tension which often resurfaces whenever two conflicting ideologies come into contact. The Greek and Roman empires were cosmopolitan places. They contained scores of nationalities, each speaking its own language and practicing its own religion. Most of the time, the ruler did not interfere in the religious affairs of his subjects. As long as they paid their taxes and kept the public order, they could worship whatever gods they chose.

Problems arose because there were certain public religious rituals in which all subjects were obliged to take part. The emperor himself was the object of a cult, as was the ruling class's pantheon of gods. Most people in the ancient world did not object and paid homage to the gods of the state. Each nation worshiped its own cluster of gods and did not deny that other gods existed for other nations. Each nation, that is, except the Jews.

''Thou shalt have no other gods before me'' is part of the Second Commandment. Judaism acknowledges the existence of only one God, creator of the universe. The gods of the pagan peoples were mere idols, lifeless blocks of wood or stone. If a Jew took part in any sort of pagan rite, he would be just as much an idol-worshipper as were the ancient Hebrews who abandoned God and worshiped the golden calf. And so the Jews of the ancient empires refused to participate in any pagan rites.

The Jews' refusal to bow down to pagan gods aroused their rulers' hostility. The Book of Esther, for example, which was written a century or so before the Maccabean revolt, tells the story of Mordecai, a Jew who refused to bow down to the wicked Haman, a symbol of idolatry. As a result:

Haman said to king Ahasuerus, ''There is a certain people, scattered and dispersed among the other peoples in all the provinces of your realm, whose laws are different from those of any other people and who do not obey the king's laws; and it is not in Your Majesty's interest to tolerate them. If it please Your Majesty, let an edict be drawn for their destruction, and I will pay ten thousand talents of silver to the stewards for deposit in the royal treasury.'' ... Accordingly, written instructions were dispatched by couriers to all the king's provinces to destroy, massacre, and exterminate all Jews, young and old, children and women, on a single day, on the thirteenth day of the twelfth month—that is, the month of Adar—and to plunder their possessions [Esther 3].

Although Haman was concerned solely with the destruction of the Jews, whereas Antiochus demanded the conversion of the Jews, Haman's speech reveals the same basic impulses and fears echoed in the Book of the Maccabees. Like Haman, Antiochus distrusted the Jews because of their separateness; he questioned their patriotism and ridiculed their faith. And as suggested by our source, Antiochus's prejudice against Jews was shared by some of the Jews themselves. There were some "renegades" who disliked feeling separate from the mainstream Greek society. They wanted to take part in that great "country club" of ancient Greek social life, the gymnasium. The fact that the gymnasium was a center for pagan worship did not stop them from wanting to join the club.

Since the time of the Maccabees, history has known many cases of individual Jews hiding their Jewishness or giving it up altogether in order to be accepted by the gentile world. But no organized Jewish group like the renegades has arisen to plot the destruction of the Jewish religion. The Maccabean revolt provoked such a strong response as to wipe out such renegade behavior forever.

As we know, the Jews responded to anti-Semitism through a successful military revolt, thus providing the Jews with religious freedom. Even in victory, however, the Jewish community continued to be surrounded by many of the Greek influences that it had set out to conquer. Although the Jews were now free to worship as they chose, it was easier to overthrow Antiochus than it was to overcome the seductive appeal of Greek culture. In other words, the Jews could offer a military response to anti-Semitism but had to develop philosophical and legal defenses against the more subtle pressures that surrounded them.

The Mishnah tells us, "Rabbi Eliezer said, 'Be diligent in learning Torah and know how to answer an Epicurean.'" (The word "Epicurean" referred to any pagan and not only followers of the Roman philosopher Epicurus.) An entire tractate of the Mishnah, *Avodah Zarah*, was composed to deal with the limits Jews should place on their contacts with gentiles:

> Three days before the feasts of the gentiles it is forbidden to do business with them, to borrow or lend to them, to pay or accept payment [on a debt]...[1:1]. The wineskins and wine-jars of idol worshippers into which a Jew's wine has entered—all of them are forbidden, and it is forbidden to derive benefit from them...The grape-seeds and grape-husks of the idol worshippers are forbidden, and it is forbidden to derive benefit from them [2:4].

Laws such as these helped to keep the Jewish people intact but at the same time strengthened the impression that Jews despised gentiles. The Jewish attempt to protect Judaism from outside influences thus led to more anti-Semitic reactions. The Roman historian Tacitus wrote:

> The Jews are extremely loyal to one another, and always ready to show compassion, but toward every other people they feel only hate and enmity. They sit apart at meals, and they sleep apart, and although as a race, they are prone to lust, they abstain from intercourse with foreign women...[Histories, 5].

Similarly, the philosopher Euphrates claimed:

. . . .[T]he Jews have long been in revolt not only against the Romans, but against humanity; and a race that has made its own life apart and irreconcilable; that can not share with mankind the pleasures of the table nor join in their libations or prayer or sacrifices, are separated from ourselves by a greater gulf than divides us from . . . the Indies [Philostratus, *Life of Apollonius*, 5:33].

Ancient literature contains many accusations that Jewish Sabbath observance was a cover-up for laziness, that the dietary laws were senseless, and that circumcision was barbaric.

The Jews did not have to look far for an answer to these slanders. For despite the hostility of propagandists like Tacitus, Judaism was an immensely popular religion in the ancient world, especially among the intellectual class. The Jewish philosopher Philo noted that Jewish laws

attract and win the attention of all, of barbarians, of Greeks, of dwellers on the mainland and islands, of nations of the east and the west, of Europe and Asia, of the whole inhabited world from end to end. For who has not shown his respect for that sacred seventh day, by giving rest and relaxation from labor to himself and his neighbors, freemen and slaves alike, and beyond these to his beasts? [Philo, *Life of Moses*, 2:17–23].

The most striking evidence of Judaism's appeal came from the Jewish historian Josephus:

There is not one city, Greek or barbarian, nor a single nation where the custom of the seventh day, on which we rest from all work, and the fasts, and the lighting of candles and our prohibitions in the matter of food are not observed . . . .What is the matter of the greatest admiration is that our law has no bait of pleasure to allure man to it, but it prevails by its own force. As God himself pervades all the world, so has our law passed through all the world also . . . .It follows, then, that our accusers must either condemn the whole world for deliberate malice in being so eager to adopt the bad laws of a foreign country in preference to the good laws of their own, or else give up their grudge against us [Josephus, *Against Apion* II:40].

It was largely the *popularity* of Judaism that led frustrated pagan scholars into spreading libels about Judaism. Roman statesmen rightly saw in Judaism a growing challenge to the religion and values of the Roman ruling class. Judaism preached a message of peace, obedience to God's law, and trust in divine justice. But ancient Rome was only as strong as her armies, and Caesar, not God, was the highest authority.

Judaism appealed to ordinary people's longing for justice and morality. Its belief in one God and the ultimate rationality of the universe also appealed to many intellectuals. Not all educated pagans shared Tacitus' disdain for the Jews. So while the leaders of Rome looked on, the Jews proselytized vigorously and increased their numbers to as much as five million, eight percent of the entire empire.

It would be wrong to leave the impression that ordinary people throughout the Roman Empire were always friendly to the Jews. Judaism appealed to many, but popular anti-Semitism also existed. On occasion, the Jews suffered the fate of being scapegoats for popular discontent. For example, in Alexandria, Egypt there was a series of riots against the Jews. But these cases were the exception, not the rule.

What do we make of this mixture of love and hatred that the ancient world displayed toward the Jews? The fact is that there was such a thing as anti-Semitism in antiquity. Jews were disliked then, as they have been throughout history, simply because they were different from other people. Xenophobia, mankind's natural fear of strangers, could feed Judeo-phobia, fear of Jews. But this fear was overpowered by the appeal of Judaism. People yearned for a goal in their life greater than service to the emperor, and for values higher than bread and circuses.

Judaism's attractive power overcame the forces of those who sought to destroy it. But a new and far more powerful form of anti-Semitism was to arise during the later history of the Roman Empire. One particular Jewish sect created a religion based on many Jewish values but opposed to Judaism as such. With the rise of Christiantiy, Judaism faced an entirely different kind of challenge from what had come before.

STUDY QUESTIONS

1 How did the differences between Judaism and other ancient religions affect the Jews' political relationships with their rulers?

2 What similarities and differences can you see between Haman's attitude and Antiochus' attitude toward the Jewish people?

3 Even before Antiochus demanded that Jewish religious practices be changed, certain Jews had already adopted pagan observances on their own. What explanations can you give for this self-motivated action?

4 What, according to our source, were the different Jewish reactions to Antiochus Epiphanes' decrees? From what you know of the story of the Maccabees, what other response did the Jews formulate? Which would you have chosen? Why?

5 What justification did the Jews give for creating the laws set forth in the Mishna tractate *avodah zarah*? How was this justification understood by the gentile world?

6 Generally speaking, what sort of people in the ancient world were hostile to Judaism, and what sort were receptive to it? Why did these different types of people react to Judaism in such different ways?

7 Compare the citations from Philo and Josephus on the popularity of Judaism. What customs in particular seem to be the most attractive? Why do you think this is so?

With the rise of the Roman Empire, the Jews faced a serious threat to the survival of their religion. This replica of the Arch of Titus depicts the Romans carrying off spoils from the Temple in Jerusalem destroyed in 70 C.E.

CHURCH VERSUS SYNAGOGUE

The Babylonian Talmud was edited around the year 500 C.E., almost two centuries after Christianity had become the official religion of the Roman Empire. Although Babylonia was not part of the Empire, the rest of the Jewish diaspora was under Roman rule. Given the Church's constant attacks against Judaism, one would think that the rabbis of the Talmud would have had a great deal to say about Christianity. But the Talmud makes no overt references to Christianity or Christians. Only thirty six of the Talmud's 15,000 pages deal with what were called *minim*—Jewish heretics—and it is not always clear if a *min* meant a Christian. Nonetheless, there are some fascinating, though cryptic, Talmudic passages about *minim* that tell us how rabbis responded to an increasingly hostile Christian world.

[Scrolls and the books of the *minim*] need not be saved from a fire. R. Jose said, "On a weekday one should cut out the names of God and lay them aside, and the rest should be burnt." R. Tarfon said, "By the life of my son, if they came into my hands I would burn them with the names of God in them. For even if a man were pursued by one who wished to kill him or by a snake who wished to bite him, it is permissable to enter a house of idol-worship to escape, but one should not enter into the houses of those [*minim*]. This is because the *minim* recognize [God] and deny [Judaism], while idol worshippers do not recognize [God] and deny [Judaism]. And of them it is written, 'You have put your memory behind the door and doorpost'" [Shabat 116a].

Rabbi Abahu said, "If someone tells you, 'I am God,' he is a liar; 'I am the son of man,' his end is that he will regret it; that 'I am going to heaven,' he says this but will not fulfill it" [Jerusalem Talmud Ta'anit 2:1].

. . . .[I]n all [biblical] passages which the *minim* have taken [to justify] their heresy, their refutation is to be found near at hand [in Scripture] [Sanhedrin 38b].

I am the Lord thy God [Ex. 20:2].—Rabbi Abahu said, "It is like a king to whom there is a father and brother; and so the Holy One says, I am not so; 'I am the first' [Is. 44:6]—I have no father—'And I am the last'—I have no brother, 'and beside me there is no God,' I have no Son" [Exodus Rabbah 29:5].

It is written: "There is one that is alone, and he has not a second; yea, he has neither son nor brother" [Eccles. 4:8]. "He has neither son nor brother," but "Hear O Israel, the Lord our God, the Lord is one" [Deuteronomy Rabbah 2:33].

R. Yehuda son of Simon [quoted the verse] "According to these words" [and interpreted them thus:] I have made a covenant with you [Moses] and with Israel. By means of what? By "Write down" and "According to these words." If you preserve that which is written written and that which is oral oral, I will make a covenant with you. Judah bar Solomon said that when God said to Moses, "Write!," Moses also requested that the Mishnah should be given in writing. But God anticipated that the gentiles would translate the Torah, read it in Greek, and say: We are Israel, and we are the children of God . . . God said to the gentiles: "You say that you are my children. I only know that [those] who possess my secret writings are my children. And what are these writings? The Mishnah" [Midrash Tanhuma, Va-Yera 5, Ki Tissa 34].

In order to explain what these texts mean, we have to backtrack from the Talmud to the early Church and its attitude toward Judaism. The first Christians considered themselves Jews, attending synagogue and observing Halacha. They differed from the Jews, however, in their messianic belief. They believed that the Messiah had already come and would return in glory; the Jews believed that the Messiah was yet to come. A generation later, however, a sort of love-hate relationship with the Jews developed. On the one hand, early Christians believed that the Jews were God's chosen people. The Jews had produced Jesus and his disciples, and Jesus' teachings were very much in keeping with that of the great Hebrew prophets. On the other hand, the Jews were despised for having rejected and persecuted Jesus:

Pilate said, "I am innocent of this man's blood. It is your concern." And all the people answered, "His blood be on us and our children!" [Matthew 27:25, 26].

As for the Torah, the foundation of Judaism, Paul taught that the Jewish Law was holy, but the Law alone had failed to keep the Jews from sin.

You preach against stealing, yet you steal; you forbid adultery, yet you commit adultery; you despise idols, yet you rob their temples. By boasting about the Law and then disobeying it, you bring God into contempt [Romans 2:22–23].

According to Paul, faith in Jesus, not the Law, would bring mankind's salvation:

But now a righteousness from God, apart from law, has been made known, to which the law and the Prophets testify. This righteousness from God comes through faith in Jesus Christ to all who believe. There is no difference, for all have sinned and fall short of the glory of God, and are justified freely by his grace through the redemption that came by Jesus Christ [Romans 3:21–4].

14

Paul claimed that he was a learned Jew who had mastered the rabbinic art of *midrash*—the interpretation of Scripture. Paul and the other early Christians combed the Jewish Scriptures for passages that allegedly predicted the coming of Jesus and proved that he was the son of God. When the Jews responded to these attacks, they claimed that Christians were twisting the true meaning of the Bible. Our texts offer examples of how the Jews came up with Biblical quotations proving that God could not be divided into a father and son, and that the Messiah had not yet come to earth.

The rabbis soon learned that their piecemeal defense against Christian attacks would not succeed, for the Christians declared the entire Jewish Bible to be a Christian holy book, an "Old Testament" that formed a prologue to the "New Testament" of Jesus and his apostles. But Judaism had an impregnable defense in its Oral Law, the Mishnah and Gemara. The Oral Law refined the written Torah into an all-embracing, uniquely Jewish system. As our last text shows, the Jews emphasized the Oral Law, glorified it, and saw in it a bulwark against Christian influences.

The rabbis feared Christian influences. The first text clearly shows that the rabbis considered Jewish Christians a greater threat to Judaism than any pagan cult. Christianity, so much of which was based in Jewish teaching, was a "fifth column" within the house of Israel. Jewish Christians continued to live, work and even worship in the Jewish community. The rabbis even had to build a device into the daily synagogue service in order to ferret out the heretics. By approximately 80 C.E. a new section was added to the Amidah, the prayer at the heart of the Jewish service. It read:

> And may there be no hope for the *minim* [heretics], and may all those who do evil be destroyed in an instant, and may they all be uprooted and torn, and the arrogant be humbled speedily. Cast them down and humble them speedily in our days. Blessed art thou, O Lord, who breakest the enemies and humbles the arrogant.

People who would not recite these lines were suspected of *minut*, or heresy.

As long as Christianity remained a Jewish sect, Christians were considered *minim*, and the rabbis had to create ways to counter their attempts to win support among the Jews. The rabbis saw little point in trying to convince the Christians of their errors; they just wanted to defend Judaism:

> R. Shmuel b. Nahman, in the name of R. Jonathon, said, "When Moses was writing the Torah, he wrote down the deeds of each day [of creation]. When he came to the verse [Gen. 1:26], 'And God said, Let us make man in our image, according to our likeness,' he said, 'O Lord of the universe! How you are giving a chance to the *minim*! I am astonished.' He said to him, 'Write; and he who will err, let him err.' " [Gen. Rabba 8:8].

By the year 80 C.E. or so, the Jews and the Christians had rejected each other completely. Rabbis excommunicated Christian groups. Jesus was dismissed by the rabbis as a rabble-rouser and a sorcerer. None of the prophesies concerning the Messiah had been fulfilled; there was still war, poverty, bigotry, and starvation:

And it is taught: On the eve of Passover they hanged Jeshu [Jesus]. And the crier went forth before him forty days, saying, "Jeshu the Nazarene is going to be stoned, because he practiced magic and deceived and led Israel astray. Any one who has anything to say in his favor, let him come forth." No one came forth in his favor. And they hanged him on the eve of Passover. Ulla says, "How could it be that Jeshu the Nazarene, a revolutionary, had anything in his favor? He was a deceiver, and the Merciful has said, *Thou shall not spare, neither shall thou conceal him*" [Deut. 13:9].

In a few decades Christianity had changed from a Jewish sect to a separate religion. Its followers were no longer Jews but converted pagans. And as Christianity changed, so did Jewish attitudes toward it. It was seen as just another form of *avodah zarah*, a pagan religion. So the rabbis adapted old Mishnaic rules regarding relations with pagans to the new situation. For example, in the Mishna, R. Meir forbids Jews from having contact with pagans three days before or after a pagan feast day. In the Talmud, Sunday, the Christian sabbath, was called a pagan feast day, and contact with Christians was forbidden three days before and after—in other words, during the whole week!

The split between the Church and the Synagogue had become a chasm. The Church branded the Jews a despised people, killers of Christ, and the Synagogue considered the Church to be a bastion of idolatry, practicing *avodah zarah*.

As Christianity changed from a Jewish sect to a separate religion appealing to converted pagans, the anti-Jewish feeling, permeating the New Testament, blossomed. Greek Christians, who had no ethnic ties to the Jews, wondered why the Jews persisted in not seeing the light. The idea spread that the Jews were not simply ignorant but, in fact, wicked; that they actually knew all along that Jesus was the Messiah but refused to accept him out of sheer spite. So anger at the Jews displaced admiration. Church fathers blackened the Jews with tirades such as these:

> [The Jews have] sacrificed their sons and daughters to devils; they outraged nature; and overthrew from their foundations the laws of relationship. They have become worse than the wild beasts, and for no reason at all, with their own hands they murder their own offspring, to worship the avenging devils who are the foes of our life."[1]

By the end of the fifth century the Jews of the Roman Empire found themselves in a Christian world that was throttling ancient Jewish privileges. Jews were prohibited from owning slaves and accepting converts. They could still own property, perform business transactions and bear arms, but the Church had made a firm decision to isolate and degrade the Jews in the hopes that they would eventually repent their wicked ways and convert.

What we have seen here is the "official" attitude of the Church and Synagogue towards each other, the "party line" as laid down by Jewish and Christian leaders. But did this official attitude really affect the way ordinary Jews and non-Jews dealt with each other? Did the typical Christian in the street despise Jews for having rejected Christ? Did a Jew shudder every time a non-Jew passed by in the street? The next chapter seeks to answer these questions.

STUDY QUESTIONS

1 How did Christian attitudes toward Jews change from the time of Paul to the fifth century? How did these changes affect the political and social status of the Jews?

2 What is a *min*? Why, according to our source from Tractate Shabat, is it a greater sin to be a *min* than an idolator?

3 Did the rabbis consider a Christian a Jew or a gentile? Why did their thinking change over time?

4 What was the rabbinic image of Jesus? Which of our sources makes reference to Jesus?

5 Why did the rabbis incorporate a curse against *minim* into the daily prayers?

6 What examples do our sources give of rabbis quoting Scripture to prove that the claims of Christianity are false? Are there cases where the rabbis admit that Scripture might seem to support Christian beliefs?

7 Locate our source from Midrash Tanhuma. According to R. Judah bar Solomon, why did God refuse to let Moses write down the Mishna? How does R. Judah's statement reflect changing Jewish conceptions of the importance of the Oral Law?

FOR DISCUSSION

Since the Holocaust, many Christians and Jews throughout the world have sought a dialogue to prevent the growth of prejudice and hatred between members of the two religions. If your were involved in a dialogue with a Christian group, how would you explain the sources presented in this chapter? Would you defend them as valid for the time they were written, or would you criticize them as intolerant? Would you support the rabbis' view of Christianity or would you develop an alternative view?

Over 300,000 Frenchmen marched under the banner of the First Crusade, begun in 1096 C.E. by Pope Urban II. Although intended to regain the Holy Land from Muslim control, the Crusade brought great destruction to those who lay in its path. By the end of the First Crusade more than 5,000 Jews had been violently murdered.

THE CRUSADES

It was the spring of 1096. Germany's Rhine Valley was filled with green fields and flowers in bloom. Little did the Jews of the valley suspect that by the end of June thousands would be dead, the victims of dreadful massacres. The Jewish chronicler Solomon ben Samson left the following account:

It was on the third of Sivan, at noon [Tuesday, May 27, 1096]... Emico [a German noble]...came with his whole army against the city gate [of Mainz, in the Rhine Valley] and the citizens opened it for him ....Then the enemies of the Lord said to each other: "Look! They have opened up the gate for us. Now let us avenge the blood of the 'hanged one' [Jesus]....

The children of the Holy Covenant who were there...young and old donned their armor and girded on their weapons....Yet because of the many troubles and the fasts which they had observed they had no strength to stand up against the enemy....Then came gangs and bands, sweeping through like a flood, until Mainz was filled from end to end.

....Panic was great in the town...Each Jew in the inner court of the bishop girded on his weapons, and all moved towards the palace gate to fight the crusaders and citizens. They fought each other up to the very gate, but the sins of the Jews brought it about that the enemy overcame them and took the gate...

The hand of the Lord was heavy against His people....The bishop's men, who had promised to help them, were the very first to flee, thus delivering the Jews into the hand of the enemy....

When the children of the Holy Covenant saw that the heavenly decree of death had been issued and that the enemy had conquered them and had entered the courtyard, then all of them...cried out together to their Father in heaven and, weeping for themselves and for their lives, accepted as just the sentence of God....With a whole heart and a willing soul they then spoke: "After all it is not right to criticize the acts of God...who has given to us His Torah and a command to put ourselves to death, to kill ourselves for the unity of His holy name. Happy are we if we do His will. Happy is anyone who is killed or slaughtered, who dies for the unity of His name, so that he is ready to enter the World to Come"....

Then all of them, to a man, cried out in a loud voice, "Let us hasten and offer ourselves as a sacrifice to the Lord. Let him who has a knife examine it that it not be nicked, and let him come and slaugher us for the sanctification of the Only One, the Everlasting, and then let him cut his own throat or plunge the knife into his own body."

... [O]ur brilliant master, Isaac ben Moses[,] ... stretched out his neck, and his head they cut off first ... The women there girded their loins with strength and slew their sons and their daughters and then themselves. Many men, too, plucked up courage and killed their wives, their sons, their infants. The tender and delicate mother slaughtered the babe she had played with; all of them, men and women arose and slaughtered one another....For the unity of the honored and awe-inspiring name were they killed and slaughtered...[2]

For almost 1000 years, Christianity was busy consolidating its hold on Europe. Little attention was paid to the Jews. During the Middle Ages the fortunes of the Jews were tied to those of the Christian Church. When the Church was weak, the Jews prospered; when Christianity grew stronger, the Jews suffered the consequences. Until the eleventh century or so, Christianity was not widely popular in Europe. True, Christianity had spread throughout the continent, but its impact was limited to a select group of people. This is why the anti-Jewish writings of the Church Fathers, which we looked at in the last chapter, did not poison the relations between Jews and non-Jews in Europe.

The good relations that prevailed between Jews and their neighbors angered a ninth-century archbishop, who complained:

No matter how kindly we treat [the Jews], we do not succeed in drawing them to the purity of our spiritual faith. On the contrary, several among us, willingly sharing with them the food of the body, have also allowed themselves to be seduced by their spiritual nourishment ....[T]he ignorant Christians claim that the Jews preach better than our own priests...Some Christians even celebrate the Sabbath with the Jews...So that the Jews might celebrate freely their Sabbath, the regional administrators have ordered the market to be transferred from Saturday to another day, leaving to the Jews even the choice of the day of the week...

Another frustrated archbishop wrote,

I have thrice publicly asked that our faithful draw aside from [the Jews], that no Christian serve them either in the cities or in the villages... I have also forbidden the eating of their food and the drinking of their liquors.[3]

Around the year 1000 C.E., the Church's intense preaching efforts began to win results. Thanks largely to itinerant monks who inspired people with their simple piety, Christianity took hold among the masses. Those same monks also convinced Europe's warrior class—the knights—to channel their fighting spirit into a holy war on behalf of Christianity. In 622 C.E. Muhammed had made his *Hegira*, his flight from Mecca to Medina, and within twenty years Islam became the dominant religion of Arabia as well as every country around it. All forms of paganism were driven out. Although Judaism and Christianity were tolerated, their followers were treated as second-class subjects. At the time of the Crusades, Israel was under Muslim rule. Taking advantage of this new spirit to fight for Christianity, the Pope called on all Christians in 1095 C.E. to join a great Crusade to free the Holy Land from Muslim rule. The call drove people into a religious frenzy. Hordes of people—nobles, knights, and peasants—answered the Pope's call. With crosses sewn on their clothes they left their homes and set out—on foot!—for Jerusalem.

Even before the call for the Crusade, the Jews had suffered from the growing militancy of Christianity. There were occasional massacres and expulsions. But the crusade to the Holy Land turned into an unprecedented bloodbath. Filled with religious zeal, the Crusaders found themselves passing through towns with Jewish communities. According to a contemporary Jewish chronicler, they thought:

> We are going on a distant journey to seek the Holy Sepulchre and to take revenge on the Ishmaelites; yet here are the Jews dwelling among us whose ancestors killed him and crucified him without reason. First let us take vengeance on them and destroy them as a people . . . .[4]

Mobs led by noblemen moved down the Rhine Valley, slaughtering as they went. They moved east to attack the Jewish communities of Bavaria and, finally, of Prague.

Most of the Jews who were killed could have been spared had they agreed to become Christians. There were Jews who did convert, although they recanted as soon as the Crusaders left. But, according to the source at the beginning of this chapter, the Jews chose to die rather than renounce their faith. Not only were they willing to die, they often chose to kill themselves rather than fall into the hands of the enemy, who might torture them into accepting baptism.

In reading the account of the massacre at Mainz, we should keep in mind that the author was not a witness. He wrote the chronicle some twenty to fifty years after the events. This does not mean that the mass suicide did not occur—there are Christian accounts that confirm many of the gruesome details. And there were several other cases of Jewish mass suicide during the Middle Ages. So the events described did take place, but how are we to understand them? How was it that Jews, whose religion hallows life and does not glorify death, came to make this ultimate sacrifice?

The Talmud teaches that if a Jew is forced to abandon his faith under threat of death, he must choose death. From the time of the Maccabees onward, Jewish history knew many martyrs who made this choice. But these were cases of individuals, not of a whole community sacrificing itself. The key to what happened in Mainz lies not only in Jewish history but also in the Christian culture that enveloped medieval Jewry.

The Jewish historian Haim Hillel Ben-Sasson has pointed out that medieval Jews lived in a world where chivalry—the knightly code of honor—was a supreme value. Death was preferable to dishonor of any sort. The Jews of Mainz, our source tell us, behaved like warriors. "Each Jew girded on his weapons" and went forth to do battle against the Crusaders. Only when the fight was lost did the Jews turn their swords upon themselves. Like a Christian knight, the Jew was willing to die nobly for his faith.

There were differences, of course, between Christian and Jewish chivalry. Although the Christian might win or lose his battle, the Jew knew he had only one option—death. The Christian idea of chivalry was aggressive, directed toward the Crusade. The Jewish ideal was directed inward, toward *kiddush ha-Shem*—the sanctification of God's name through death.

The ideal of *kiddush ha-Shem* became fixed in the medieval Jewish imagination as it had during the rebellions against Rome a millenium before, when Jews had submitted to torture and to death rather than relinquish the Torah. The death of men, women and children was considered a sacrifice like those offered to God in the ancient Temple in Jerusalem. Hebrew hymns of that time, called *piyuttim*, return over and over to the image of Abraham offering up his son Isaac. Just as God demanded that Abraham sacrifice his son as test of faith, so God was now testing the Jews. David Bar Meshulam wrote:

> ...Tender children and women gave themselves up to the binding, like choice lambs in the Temple. O Only One, Lofty One, we are pierced and murdered for Your sake, for refusing to bow our heads before the children of wantonness...
>
> Once, long ago, we could rely upon the merit of Abraham's sacrifice at Mount Moriah, that it would safeguard us and bring salvation age after age. But now one sacrifice follows another, they can no longer be counted. O Living God, may the merit of their righteousness protect us and call a halt to our miseries!

The idea of *kiddush ha-Shem* sustained the Jews throughout the long, dark centuries that followed the First Crusade. As long as the Jews believed that there was some purpose for their suffering, they could bear it. But although the Jews' faith did not waver, Jews agonized over God's apparent indifference to their prayers for comfort and revenge:

> My God, I cling to You, like a drowning man struggling to reach land. How good to be joined to You! I have always wrapped myself in Your Name, even though because of You I have been slaughtered. I have fought God's fight. *Be not far from me!*...

> Remember the massacre I suffered for Your sake. So many of us perished. Yet morning and evening and at noon Your loyal servants acclaim Your Oneness with all their hearts. This is the people that survived the sword. *Be not far from me!*...

> Lift up Your hand, set the beast on fire, hurl it into the depths of the abyss, destroy it. It has lured me into servitude, and thus subjected me to every kind of punishment. Is Your arm too short to redeem? *Be not far from me!*

Most telling of all is Ephraim of Regensburg's plaintive cry:

> My God, my God, why are my sighs hidden from You? I am nothing but a helpless dove.[5]

The Jews suffered horribly during the Crusades which continued into the twelfth and thirteenth centuries. Unfortunately, the degradation of European Jewry had only begun. The violent anti-Semitism unleashed by the Crusades was just beginning to run its course.

STUDY QUESTIONS

1 How did medieval Christian attitudes toward Jews change during the period before the Crusades? How, according to the *piyuttim* cited at the end of the chapter, did the Jewish attitudes towards Christians change after the Crusades?

2 What particular principle or belief did the Jews of Mainz invoke in justifying their mass suicide? Why was this principle so important to them?

3 Why did the Jews of Mainz consider suicide their only viable option? Do you think it was appropriate?

4 What Biblical event became the model for medieval acts of *kiddush ha-Shem*? In what crucial way did the Biblical event differ from the case of a Jew submitting to death?

5 What do the *piyuttim* tell us about medieval Jewish feelings about God?

6 Look back to our source in chapter one. What difference do you see between the mass suicide of the Jews of Mainz and the Jewish martyrdom under the persecution of Antiochus Epiphanes?

7 What was chivalry? How did the Jews absorb Christian ideas of chivalry? How did the Jews alter them, and why?

FOR DISCUSSION

Our source brings up a basic historical problem. We rely heavily on documents such as the one by Solomon ben Samson when trying to recreate past events. But how do we know that a document is telling the truth? What reason do we have for believing that Solomon ben Samson accurately reported the story of the Jews of Mainz? According to the commentary, which factors cast doubt on his story, and which support it? Consider the relationship between the *piyuttim* and the despair they express with the stoic attitude of the Jews before they died as described by Solomon ben Samson. Do you personally find Solomon ben Samson's account believable? Why or why not?

In an attempt to weaken the Jewish religious strength, the Church tried to eliminate the Talmud. If the Talmud was found to contain anti-Christian passages it could be confiscated and burned. The engraving above pictures a disputation in which Jews and Christians quote Biblical passages to support their opposing argument.

TRIAL AND EXILE

In Europe, during the late Middle Ages, the Jewish religion was literally put on trial for its life. The popes and kings of Christendom summoned Jews to disputations where the teachings of Judaism came under vicious attack. One such disputation took place in Barcelona in 1263 C.E. The accusers were King James I of Aragon, the Dominican leader Raymund de Pennaforte, and Pablo Christiani, a Jewish convert. The defender was Spain's greatest rabbi, Moses ben Nahman, known as Nahmanides. The following passage is taken from a Hebrew account of the disputation believed to have been written by Nahmanides himself.

[The disputation began with Christian arguments that within the Talmud itself lay proof that Jesus was the Messiah. Nahmanides responded:] "My lord King, hear me. The Messiah is not fundamental to our religion. Why, you are worth more to me than the Messiah! You are a king; and he is a king. You are a Gentile king, and he is a Jewish king; for the Messiah is only a king of flesh and blood like you. When I serve my creator in your territory in exile and affliction and servitude and reproach of the peoples who 'reproach us continually,' my reward is great. For I am offering a sacrifice to God from my body, by which I shall be found more and more worthy of the life of the world to come. But when there will be a king of Israel of my religion ruling over all the peoples, and there will be no choice for me but to remain in the Jewish religion, my reward will not be so great. No, the real point of difference between Jews and Christians lies in what you say about the fundamental matter of the deity; a doctrine which is distasteful indeed. You, our lord King, are a Christian and the son of a Christian, and you have listened all your life to priests who have filled your brain and the marrow of your bones with this doctrine, and it has settled with you, because of that accustomed habit. But the doctrine in which you believe, and which is the foundation of your faith, cannot be accepted by the reason, and nature affords no grounds for it, nor have the prophets ever expressed it. Nor can even the miraculous stretch as far as this, as I shall explain with full proofs in the right time and place, that the Creator of heaven and earth resorted to the womb of a certain Jewess and grew there for nine months and was born as an infant, and afterwards grew up and was betrayed into the hands of his enemies who sentenced him to death and executed him, and that afterwards, as you say, he came to life and returned to his original place. The mind of a Jew, or any other person, cannot tolerate this; and you speak your words entirely in vain, for this is the root of our controversy. Nevertheless, let us speak of the Messiah too, as this is your wish.''

Said [Brother Pablo Christiani], ''Will you believe, then, that he has come?''

Said I, ''No. On the contrary, I believe and know that [the Messiah] has not come . . . The prophet says that in the time of the Messiah, . . . 'The earth shall be full of the knowledge of the Lord, as the waters cover the sea.' [Isaiah 11:9]; also, 'They shall beat their swords into ploughshares . . . nation shall not lift up sword against nation, neither shall they learn war any more.' [Isaiah 2:4]. Yet from the days of Jesus until now, the whole world has been full of violence and plundering, and the Christians are greater spillers of blood than all the rest of the peoples, and they are also practisers of adultery and incest. And how hard it would be for you, my lord King, and for your knights, if they were not to learn war any more! . . .

[The King] said, ''Let the disputation be discontinued, for I have never seen a man who was in the wrong argue as well as you did . . . Return to your city in life and peace.[6]

At first glance, the issues raised and the methods used at Barcelona seem no different from what we saw in the chapter on the early Church. The monks quote Scripture to prove that Jesus was the Messiah, and the rabbi counters with quotations to show that he was not. But the Dominicans at Barcelona were actually far more sophisticated, and so more threatening, than their predecessors. They launched a war against the Talmud itself. At Barcelona and at other disputations the Church used passages from the Talmud to prove the truth of Christianity. Even more damaging were Jewish converts to Christianity who pointed out to the Church anti-Christian passages like those we looked at in chapter two. These passages prompted Pope Gregory IX to write in 1239 C.E.:

> If what is said about the Jews of France and of the other lands is true, no punishment would be sufficiently worthy of their crime. For they, so we have heard, are not content with the Old Law which God gave to Moses in writing; they even ignore it completely, and affirm that God gave another Law which is called 'Talmud', that is 'Teaching', handed down to Moses orally. . . . In this is contained matter so abusive and unspeakable that it arouses shame in those who mention it and horror in those who hear it.[7]

The Talmud emerged unscathed from the Barcelona disputation, although Nahmanides had to flee Spain to escape persecution. The outcome of events, however, did not always turn out so well. After a disputation in Paris in 1240 C.E. King Louis IX seized and burned cartloads of the Talmud and other Jewish manuscripts. In 1413 C.E. another disputation in Spain led to widespread censorship of the Talmud. Whole sections were erased under the heavy hand of the Spanish Inquisition. To this day, a truly correct text of the Talmud is almost impossible to establish because of the centuries of censorship and actual destruction of manuscripts.

This assault on the Talmud was just one sign of a steady growth of anti-Semitism in the late Middle Ages. The problem facing the Jews was that they were coming under attack from both the masses and the elite in Christendom. Before Christianity had really taken hold in Europe, anti-Semitism was limited to the clergy. In time, however, Christianity became widely accepted, resulting in the mob-led massacres of the Crusades. The folk imagination brewed up a wild, demonic image of the Jews. Jews were accused of ritual murder against Christians, poisoning wells, and all forms of witchcraft.

Some kings and popes tried to protect the Jews against the mobs, but most failed. The kings of England, France and Spain expelled the Jews from their lands. The kings would borrow money from the Jews and then drive them out. The Pope and the German Emperor had the Jews restricted to ghettos. Throughout Europe, church and state conspired to force the Jews out of commerce and craft guilds.

How did the Jews survive this terrible ordeal? For many, the only answer was to find more hospitable lands. Masses of Jews moved from the hostile lands of Western and Central Europe into Poland, where anti-Semitism was weak and Jews were accepted as merchants. Jews expelled from Spain were welcomed into the Ottoman Empire. The Jews did more, however, than migrate physically. Spiritually and philosophically they also sought new avenues of thought through which to deal with their persecution and forced migration.

Jewish thinkers saw themselves as the defenders of the true faith in a dark and superstitious world. The fact that Jews were persecuted only proved that the world was not yet worthy of God's teaching. At Barcelona, Nahmanides plainly states his disdain for Christian doctrine. He considers it irrational and unbelievable. The teachings of Judaism, on the other hand, are acceptable to any educated mind. This proud assertion is echoed over and over again in the writings of Maimonides and other great medieval Jewish philosophers. At the time of the Protestant Reformation, when bible-toting zealots eagerly sought the conversion of the Jews, one contemporary rabbi warned:

> Do not begin with a disputation with them by quoting passages from the Bible, *but only by way of nature, the heart, and reason.* One has to believe, and there must be a unity which directs the entire Universe . . . And this is what you should do to purify and refine them and talk to them—suppose there were no Bible in existence, what could we do? . . . For their faith is based on our Prophets and Holy Scriptures, and if we have no Prophets, they have no proof to present . . . But we have a principle and foundation even without any Book of Scripture, and that is in nature: that we believe in God's unity and greatness from His every activity; and because whatever is done every day could not be done save by His Will.[8]

Jewish views of Christians became a mirror image of Christian attitudes about the Jews. Judaism was the "true" religion and Christianity "false." Jews thought of Christians as corrupt, wicked people, best avoided as much as possible. Many interesting warnings about Christians are found in the *Sefer Hasidim* (Book of the Pious), edited in Germany in the thirteenth century. One section reads:

In a certain city there was no sufficient water for immersing, but the area was spacious, and the Jews wanted to live there. But the [rabbi] said, "Since the only water there is water into which thieves and priests have entered, and they invoke therein their idol worship, it will not be possible for women to immerse in it. And if one immerses knives and metal and glass objects into that water, it will not be proper to recite a blessing in which mentions the name of God" [Para. 439, Maraglit ed].

The "ordeal by water" described in the *Sefer Hasidim* refers to the practice of casting accused criminals into the river. Their guilt or innocence was determined by whether they floated or sank. In this account, the river of the town literally threatened to contaminate the Jews. The Jews had to be ever watchful to maintain their purity. We see from the story that the Jews turned Christian persecution into a challenge, a great contest to see if they would hold up under the obstacles placed before them.

Although degraded, the Jews could hold their heads high. Israel was like a jewel encrusted with dirt. In the days of the Messiah, the Jews believed the jewel would once again shine in all its splendor. But they yearned to know when that time would come and why the Messiah had tarried for so long. For Jews awash in misery, talk about the superiority of Judaism brought little comfort. Constant persecution awakened another Jewish response, less rational, more plaintive. This was the idea of *galut*, exile.

When Nahmanides debated the Dominicans at Barcelona he sounded cool, almost indifferent, when he talked about the Messiah. Perhaps he was trying to point out the Jewish emphasis on *this* world in contrast to the medieval Christian obsession with the "heavenly kingdom"; perhaps he was insinuating that the Christian "Messiah" had done little to bring about a true Messianic age. But despite his professed indifference when speaking to Christians, Nahmanides—like other Jews of his time—must have longed for the coming of the Messianic age that would bring an end to Jewish suffering in Christian Europe and a gathering of all Jews to the Land of Israel.

Nahmanides himself undertook the hazardous pilgrimage to the Holy Land, as did the greatest Jewish poet of the middle ages, Yehuda ha-Levi. Listen to this lament, written by ha-Levi as Christian armies were advancing on his native Muslim Spain:

O Zion, will you not ask how your captives are—the exiles who seek your welfare, who are the remnant of your flocks? From west to east, north and south, from every side, accept the greetings of those near and far, and the blessings of this captive of desire, who sheds his tears like the dew of Hermon and longs to have them fall upon your hills. I am like a jackal when I weep for your affliction; but when I dream of your exiles' return I am a lute for your songs...

If only I could roam through those places where God was revealed to your prophets and heralds! Who will give me wings, so that I may wander far away? I would carry the pieces of my broken heart over your rugged mountains. I would bow down, my face on your ground; I would love your stones; your dust would move me to pity. I would weep, as I stood by my ancestors' graves, I would grieve, in Hebron, over the choicest of burial places! I would walk in your forests and meadows, stop in Gilead, marvel at Mount Abarim; Mount Abarim and Mount Hor, where the two great luminaries [Moses and Aaron] rest, those who guided you and gave you light. The air of your land is the very life of the soul, the grains of your dust are flowing myrrh, your rivers are honey from the comb. It would delight my heart to walk naked and barefoot among the desolate ruins where your shrines once stood; where your Ark was hidden away, where your cherubim once dwelled in the innermost chamber. I shall cut off my glorious hair and throw it away, I shall curse Time that has defiled your pure ones in the polluted lands . . . .[9]

The Jew seeking relief from persecution yearned for the Holy Land. Small bands of Jews actually moved there; most merely dreamed about it.

It is ironic that medieval anti-Semitism, which caused the Jews such misery, actually helped strengthen the Jewish spirit. Disputations and degradation deepened the Jews' belief in the supremacy of the Torah. Ceaseless persecution confirmed the feeling that the Jews were living in *galut*, a state of defilement and loss. This was the legacy of the Jewish encounter with medieval Christendom.

STUDY QUESTIONS

1 What was the Church's motive behind commanding Jews to come to disputations? What was the usual result of these disputations?

2 What effect did these disputations have on popular attitudes toward the Jews? What other events of the late Middle Ages helped worsen anti-Semitism in Europe?

3 What proof did Nahmanides offer during the Barcelona Disputation that the Messiah had not come? Do you think a believing Christian would find his argument convincing? Why or why not?

4 In our source, does Nahmanides give the impression that Jews eagerly await the coming of the Messiah? Do other sources cited in the chapter confirm or deny Nahmanides' statement?

5 Nahmanides and other medieval Jewish thinkers asserted that Judaism was a religion of reason and that Christian doctrine was based only on superstition. How did Nahmanides support this belief? Does this argument strike you as sound? Why or why not?

6 What physical response did Jews offer to the persecutions of the late Middle Ages?

7 What does the excerpt from *Sefer Hasidim* tell us about Jewish feelings about Christians during the late Middle Ages?

FOR DISCUSSION

Consider the following argument:

According to Yehuda ha-Levi, the Jews live in exile (*galut*). *Galut* has both physical and spiritual aspects. *Galut* is physical in that Jews are separated from the land which God provided for them. The Holy Land is in ruins, and no ordinary Jewish life can go on there now. But even if the Jews were to return to Palestine and rebuild it into a thriving country, there would still be a *spiritual* form of exile. Since the destruction of the Temple, God's presence has departed from the world. He has turned his face away from His chosen people. Only reconciliation with God will bring about a true end to the exile.

Some people have called Yehuda ha-Levi a forerunner of Zionism. Do you agree? Do his views differ from your own conceptions of Zionism?

The effects of living under Islamic rule extended far beyond religious matters. Jewish art and architecture were greatly influenced by the Islamic culture. Built in Toledo, Spain, the Shushan Synagogue pictured here is reflective of the Moorish architecture during the fourteenth century.

DAR AL-ISLAM

In 1172 the greatest Jewish scholar of the Middle Ages, Moses Maimonides, received shocking news from the leaders of the Jews of Yemen. Hard times had fallen on this ancient Jewish community. A fanatical Muslim leader was persecuting the Jews, forcing them to convert to Islam under pain of death. Desolate and dispirited, some of the Jews had found comfort in a false Messiah who was wandering throughout the country. Maimonides responded to the Yemenites' lament with an uplifting, inspiring letter. It was intended mainly to warn the Yemenites to stay away from any involvement with false Messiahs. (In the past, such people had provoked the anger of the Muslim authorities, with dire consequences for the Jewish communities.) But in a more general way, the letter sought to make some sense out of the Yemenite Jews' suffering and to explain the position of the Jews in the Muslim world—*dar al-Islam*.

> You have mentioned the affair of this rebel who has arisen in the land of Yemen and who has decreed forced apostasy upon Israel, compelling people in all the places that have come under his sway to abandon the Faith, just as the Berbers in the Maghreb [northwestern Africa]. This news has broken our backs and has stunned and bewildered all of our community. . . .[M]y brethren, you must all hearken to what I am about to say to you and carefully reflect upon it . . . Verily, [Judaism] is the authentic religion of truth. . . .Through it, God has distinguished us from all the rest of mankind . . . Because He has singled us out by His laws and precepts, and because our preeminence has been established over all others by His statutes and ordinances, all the nations have risen up against us out of envy for our religion and a desire to suppress it . . . .
>
> [The Jews' worst enemies are those who] lay claim to prophecy and to bring forth a religious law contrary to the word of God, while asserting that it too was from God just like the true Word.
>
> The first to take up this course was Jesus the Nazarene—may his bones be ground to dust. He was of Israel.
>
> Later there arose a madman [Muhammad][10] who followed his example since he had paved the way for him. However, he added a further object, namely to seek dominion and complete submission to himself; and what he has established is well known . . . .

We have already received a warning concerning the present danger from God Exalted through [the prophet] Daniel that at some future time there would arise a man who would bring a religion resembling the true faith. He would come with a scripture and an oral tradition. He would make grandiose claims, namely, that his scripture was revealed to him from heaven, and that he conversed with God, as well as many other statements....

The Exalted One, Whose Name is Glorious, revealed [in the seventh and eighth chapters of the biblical book of Daniel] that He would destroy that man [Muhammad] after he had attained greatness and longstanding power, and with him those followers of his predecessor [Jesus] who still remained.

God Exalted promised the Patriarch Jacob that even if his descendants were humiliated and subjected by the nations, they would live on after them and survive them.

God Exalted has assured us via the prophets that we shall not perish, we shall not be annihilated....Therefore...do not let any series of persecutions, or the victory of enemies over us, or the weakness of our prestige, dismay you....Therefore, all of our brethren of Israel scattered in the Diaspora must encourage one another. The elder should guide the younger, and the elite the masses....

You know, my brethren, that on account of our sins God has cast us into the midst of this people, the nation of Ishmael, who persecute us severely, and who devise ways to harm us and to debase us. This is as the Exalted had warned us: "Even our enemies themselves being judges" [Deut. 32:31]. No nation has ever done more harm to Israel. None has matched it in debasing and humiliating us. None has been able to reduce us as they have....We have borne their imposed degredation, their lies and absurdities, which are beyond human power to bear....We have done as our sages of blessed memory have instructed us, bearing the lies and absurdities of Ishmael. Listen, but remain silent....[11]

Until modern times, more Jews lived in the domain of Islam than in the domain of Christianity. The Middle East and North Africa were the homelands of the majority of the world's Jews. As our text shows, the Jews of Islam, like the Jews of Christendom, suffered discrimination and persecution.

Muhammad considered Jews and Christians to be "people of the Book," people to whom God had revealed Himself through prophets and Scripture. Muhammad also considered himself to be the last and greatest prophet, who had received God's final revelation. So Muhammad was willing to tolerate "people of the Book" under the rule of Islam—but only as the inferiors of the "true believers," the Muslims. The Koran commands the believers to fight against the Jews and Christians "until they pay tribute out of hand and are utterly subdued." [9:29]. "People of the Book" were made to promise:

We shall not hold any public religious ceremonies. We shall not seek to proselytize anyone. We shall not prevent any of our kind from embracing Islam if they so desire. We shall show deference to the Muslims and shall rise from our seats when they wish to sit down. We shall not attempt to resemble the Muslims in any way with regard to their dress ....We shall not speak as they do....[12]

In return for these concessions, Jews and Christians became protected minorities, known as *dhimmis*.

Jews and Christians received equal treatment under Islamic law. But one could argue that Islam had a more hostile attitude toward Judaism than toward Christianity. This can be seen even during Muhammad's lifetime, when Jewish tribes in the Arabian desert were often at war with the Muslims. Muhammad did not have the same kind of belligerent contact with Christians, so he formed the opinion that:

> You will find that the most implacable of men in their enmity to the faithful are the Jews and the pagans, and that the nearest in love to those who believe [in Islam] are those who say, 'We are Christians'. That is because there are priests and monks among them; and because they are free from pride [Koran 5:82].

Despite this tension, Judaism held up under Islam far better than Christianity. Christianity, the religion of kings and emperors, did not adjust well to *dhimmi* status. Judaism, however, held on strong. The Jews were used to being a subject people; they had first endured captivity a thousand years before Muhammad! The Jews thus clung to their faith although surrounded by the ever-growing realm of Islam. This is not to say that Jews never converted to Islam; but this was the exception not the rule. According to one medieval Jewish writer:

> [T]o this day, we never see anyone converting to Islam unless in terror, or in quest of power, or to avoid heavy taxation, or to escape humiliation, or if taken prisoner, or because of infatuation with a Muslim woman, or for some similar reason. Nor do we see a respected, wealthy and pious non-Muslim well versed in both his faith and that of Islam going over to the Islamic faith without some of the aforementioned or similar motives.[13]

Jews were the most obvious minority in the Islamic world, and a stubborn one at that. They lived at the mercy of Muslim society. When the conditions were right and the public mood tolerant, the Jews flourished. But in times of social tension or political crisis the Jews could be made to suffer as they had in Christian Europe.

Let us look at two extremes. From the tenth to the twelfth centuries the Jews of Muslim Spain achieved power as they had never done before. Jewish generals and statesmen succeeded in politics while Jewish poets succeeded in art. Consider the lighthearted verse of the Spanish Jew Moses ibn Ezrah, who cajoles us to:

> Plunge your heart into pleasures, make merry, drink out of wine-skins by the riverside to the sound of lyres, doves, and swifts; dance and rejoice, clap your hands, get drunk and knock on the door of the lovely girl![14]

Unfortunately for ibn Ezrah, his party was doomed to come to a tragic end. In 1066 there was a pogrom against the Jews of his native Grenada. In 1090 the Jewish community was razed again, but this time by invaders, not the local population.

This was only the beginning. A dreadful fanaticism began to affect the world of Islam around the end of the twelfth century. A Berber tribe called the Almohade took power in North Africa and much of Spain. The Almohades were fiercely intolerant of infidels. As in Yemen, there were cases of forced conversion. It was this dark side of Muslim-Jewish relations that was in Maimonides' mind as he wrote the epistle to the Jews of Yemen.

Maimonides was worried lest Islam win the loyalty of Jews weary of persecution and humiliation. After all, some elements of Islam, with its strict adherence to monotheism, were not so different from Judaism. Like Judaism, Islam was based on scripture and prophecy. There was nothing in its doctrine as offensive to Judaism as the Christian idea of the incarnation of God in human form. So Maimonides' letter stressed the falseness of Muhammad's claim to prophesy. It asserted that the Jews would not be destroyed but would outlive all their enemies.

Maimonides was less than fair in describing Jewish life under Islam as having been one of constant persecution. Not only in Spain, but elsewhere during the Middle Ages, the Jews of Islam usually led comfortable, secure lives. However, Maimonides' letter did predict what would happen to the Jews in the modern Islamic world. The Ottoman Empire, which injected new life into the Middle East when it was founded in the fifteenth century, began to decay in the seventeenth century. As the Empire crumbled, the position of the Jews deteriorated. The historian Bernard Lewis has written, "Loss of power led to loss of confidence, and this in turn to a loss of tolerance."[15] Long-forgotten anti-Jewish laws were brutally enforced; new ones were enacted. The ghetto—the *mellah*—made its grim appearance in the Arab world. Grinding poverty and public degradation became inescapable parts of Jewish life in the modern Middle East.

"We listen and remain silent," Maimonides said to the Jews of Yemen. Ottoman Jewry accepted its fate and wrapped itself ever more tightly into its faith. As an eighteenth-century visitor to Aleppo, Syria, observed:

> In general, the Jews are a more sober people than the Christians. Many of them are secured from intemperance by poverty, besides which, their attendance twice a day at the synagogue on all festivals, and their living so much under the eye of their Khakhans [that is, their *hakhamim*, rabbis], render it more difficult to conceal debauchery, than it would among a more numerous nation. The lower people live chiefly on bread, pulse, herbs, and roots, dressed with the expressed oil of sesamum, which is seldom eaten by the other inhabitants. They consume more poultry than any other animal food....Their meat is sold to their poor at an under price, the difference being made up to the seller out of the national chest...[16]

We see the same patterns in this account of nineteenth-century Cairo:

> The Jews in Egypt generally lead a very quiet life: indeed, they find few but persons of their own religion who will associate with them. Their diet is extremely gross; but they are commonly regarded as a sober people. The more wealthy among them dress handsomely at home; but put on a plain or even shabby dress before they go out ....They are careful, by every means in their power, to avoid the suspicion of being possessed of much wealth. It is for this reason that

they make so shabby a figure in public, and neglect the exterior appearance of their houses.[17]

Western European travelers to the Middle East in the nineteenth century were shocked by the poverty and decay that confronted them. Those who wandered into the Jewish quarters encountered a way of life quite different from that of the Jews back home in Europe. Throughout Europe the ghetto walls were coming down; the bonds of Jewish serfdom were loosening. The Jews of Europe, unlike their brethren in the Middle East, could look confidently ahead to a new era of freedom and dignity. Anti-Semitism, so they thought, would soon be a thing of the past.

STUDY QUESTIONS

1 What was Muhammad's policy toward Jews and Christians? Did he feel the same toward members of both religions? Did he consider one of the two faiths closer to his own? Why or why not?

2 What is a *dhimmi*? How did the status of a Jew in Islam compare with that of a Jew living in Christendom? In which of the two realms, do you think, was a Jew better off?

3 In Maimonides' letter to the Jewish Yemenite community Maimonides refers to the book of Daniel, chapters seven and eight, as a means of understanding the present situation in Islam. Why was the book of Daniel so important to Maimonides in responding to the problems facing the Jews in Islam?

4 What grounds did Maimonides have to fear that Jews would convert to Islam? According to other sources in this chapter, was conversion, in fact, common? Why or why not?

5 At what time in history did the Jews of Islam enjoy the greatest prestige? The worst oppression? What connection do you see between the political rise and fall of the Islamic world and its treatment of Jews?

6 According to the reports of travelers at the end of the chapter, what effect did oppression have on Middle Eastern Jews' social and cultural life? What defenses did these Jews create to ward off anti-Semitic attack?

FOR DISCUSSION

Some people in Israel argue that given the bias in Islamic Law against Jews, there is no reason for Arabs in Israel to expect anything better than second-class treatment themselves. Does this argument strike you as reasonable? Moral? What political consequences could such thinking bring? What conception of Jewish obligations toward non-Jews underlies this argument? Do you have an alternative view?

NAPOLÉON LE GRAND,

rétablit le culte des Israélites, le 30 Mai 1806.

Une antique nation, autrefois l'unique dépositaire des volontés du Très haut, et gouvernée par la divine législation de Moïse, est dispersée depuis plus de dix-sept Siècles sur la surface du globe. En rapport avec tous les Peuples, elle ne se mêle avec aucun, et elle semble exister pour voir passer devant elle le torrent des siècles qui les entraine. Un tel phénomène serait inexplicable, s'il ne tenait qu'à l'ordre politique, car il était moralement impossible que les Juifs pussent longtems exister, malgré toutes les vicissitudes et les persécutions dont ils furent les victimes chez les différentes nations de la terre. Dans combien de proscriptions ne furent-ils pas envelloppés? Pour ne parler que de la France, qui ne sait les haines, les mépris, les outrages, les confiscations, les bannissemens, les supplices même qu'ils y ont endurés? rien de cruel, rien de deshonorant ne leur a été épargné; de sorte que l'on serait tenté de croire que nos aïeux ne les comptaient point au nombre des humains. En vain quelques orateurs éloquens s'élevèrent contre une si criante injustice, leur voix ne fut point entendue, et les infortunés Israélites paraissaient à jamais condamnés à l'avilissement et à l'opprobre. Un nouveau Cyrus a paru, mais il a fait pour eux plus que l'ancien. S'il n'a pas reconstruit leur temple, il leur a donné une patrie et des lois protectrices de leur culte et de leurs droits civils; en les rendant citoyens et membres de la grande nation, il leur a rendu l'honneur; en leur donnant des mœurs, il les a garantis pour jamais du mépris de ses peuples. Pénétrés de reconnaissance pour de si précieux bienfaits, les enfans d'Israël se sont prosternés au pied du trône du Grand Napoléon, et les filles de Sion ont fait retentir les voûtes des temples de ces cantiques célèbres que répétaient les échos du Jourdain, lorsqu'au retour de sa captivité le peuple Hébreu célébrait les miséricordes du Seigneur. La gratitude des Israélites français ne s'est pas bornée à de simples démonstrations, ils prouvent chaque jour qu'ils sont dignes des faveurs du Souverain par leur attachement à son auguste personne et par leur soumission à ses loix.

Hoping to make the Jews loyal subjects of France, Napoleon granted them full citizenship. For the first time since the days of Rome, Jews were given the same rights and privileges as the people among whom they lived.

EMANCIPATION

Moritz Lazarus was a celebrated anthropologist and Jewish communal leader in nineteenth-century Germany. In 1880, as a wave of anti-Semitism swept the German Empire, Lazarus organized an assembly of Jewish leaders in Berlin. Here is an excerpt from his speech to that assembly.

Now, gentlemen, many of us say, there is no danger. What do you consider a danger? That our rights as citizens will be seriously threatened? No, certainly not! I am confident that that would not happen in Germany and Prussia....[w]e are hurt [by anti-Semitism] much more as Germans than as Jews. It is as Germans that we feel the disgrace of the German nation in the eyes of the world.

What is to be done?...You must create an organization, which works for you, which advises and acts. You must create an organization...a central point for the ideal tasks of the Jews in Germany, for those ideal tasks...which they as Jews can accomplish in the service of the fatherland. And these ideal tasks [are]: 1. Defense against agitation raised against us, against tolerance and humanity. 2. The elevation of Judaism both in our eyes and in those of others. Many Jews have become somewhat removed from Judaism. They are not armed with knowledge of the specific value, the special advantages, the unique spiritual treasures of Judaism. We have to ensure the progress of Judaism and our awareness of it....

I freely admit that there are many among us who reject this idea from both sides. The one finds progress in Judaism absolutely unnecessary. They even deny that there has been such a thing, although one can show it to them as an historic fact. As to the others—Judaism doesn't interest them, so why should they be concerned with its progress? They are only Jews because they were born that way. They are outraged because they feel so blameless in this [anti-Semitic] agitation. They weren't even Jews, and now they are, and they have to suffer for it! They are only Jews by the grace of Stoecker.[18] We can't accomplish anything with these two types. For all those who are only Jews because they were born that way, Judaism is indeed only a misfortune.[19] For those who are willing to be Jews in the spirit, it is a source of pride. A source of pride, because it is a calling. Throughout history, each people has had its special calling; Judaism has one as well ....

39

3. We must ensure not only an elevation of Judaism but an elevation of the Jews....Whatever we do in the field of defense and explanation [to non-Jews], we ourselves must at the same time undergo moral elevation.....

We work...directly for the fatherland, in its service and in its interests, when we strive for the strengthening of the sense of community in order to promote our moral power. The elevation of the moral power of the citizens benefits the fatherland above all else, for we as a community and as individuals have no higher purpose than that of the fatherland....[20]

Lazarus wrote these lines more than a half century before Hitler rose to power in Germany. We who live many decades after the Holocaust find it hard to imagine a time when German Jews felt love for their country and hope for the future. But the nineteenth century was such a time. Jews in Germany knew that an anti-Semitic virus had attacked the German body politic, but they firmly believed that it would eventually weaken and die.

Some historical background will put Lazarus' remarks in their proper context. The period from approximately 1790 to 1870 is known as the era of emancipation—the time when Jews were granted citizenship and legal rights throughout Europe. Jewish emancipation was fueled by the fervor of social enlightenment and the great democratic revolutions of the era, the American in 1776 and the French in 1789. The motto of the French Revolution, "Liberty, equality, fraternity," pointed to the belief that all people deserve equal rights. Jews could thus claim the same rights enjoyed by everyone else—no more, no less. In order to become citizens, Jews were required to give up control of their own communal life, a control that they had enjoyed for centuries. In addition, the Jews were pressured to relinquish their unique culture and sense of peoplehood.

Many Jews accepted the price of emancipation. The French Jewish historian Theodor Reinach wrote in 1881:

> ...the Jews, since they have ceased to be pariahs, must identify themselves, in heart and in fact, with the nations which have accepted them, renounce the practices, the aspirations, the peculiarities of costume, of language which tended to isolate them from their fellow citizens, in a word cease to be a dispersed nation, and henceforth be considered only a religious denomination.[21]

It is clear from our text that Lazarus considered himself completely German and a true-blooded patriot. Jews in France, Austria, England and the United States felt the same kind of patriotism for their own homelands. Jews served proudly in their nations' armies and fought one another in battle.

A German Jew like Lazarus had good reason to feel loyalty toward Germany. Germany had a large thriving Jewish community. German Jews enjoyed much more freedom than those in the Russian Empire. The German Empire offered not only political freedom but economic and educational opportunities as well. German Jews were among the most affluent and best-educated Jews in the world.

Jewish freedom and prosperity, however, were in grave jeopardy. They were threatened by exactly the same forces that had led to emancipation in the first place. Jews were emancipated with the expectation that they would give up all signs of their Jewishness. Those Jews who refused to do so were accused of remaining a separate people, a "state within a state." Those who tried to assimilate completely were hated even more. According to the German philosopher Karl Eugen Duehring:

> A Jewish question would still exist, even if every Jew were to turn his back on his religion and join one of our major churches....It is precisely the baptized Jews who infiltrate furthest, unhindered in all sectors of society and political life....[T]he Jews are to be defined solely on the basis of race...[22]

This racial anti-Semitism struck roots throughout Europe and, to a lesser degree, in the United States. It was particularly strong in Germany. It infected every aspect of German culture. The German composer Richard Wagner was a vicious anti-Semite. He wrote:

> The Jew...strikes us primarily by his outward appearance, which, no matter to what European nationality we belong, has something disagreeably foreign to that nationality; instinctively, we wish to have nothing in common with a man who looks like that....[23]

Anti-Semitism had developed a new motif. In the modern world, where religion did not weigh on people's minds as it had during the Middle Ages, Jews were not despised solely because of their religion. Rather, they were hated for qualities that their enemies considered ingrained into the Jewish character. The word "anti-Semitism" is itself a sign of this new kind of Jewish hatred. The word was coined in 1879 by a German journalist named Wilhelm Marr, who considered Jews members of an inferior, "semitic" race.

Christian anti-Judaism still lurked in the back of people's minds, but it found different forms of expression. Take, for example, the French philosopher Voltaire, the symbol of the eighteenth-century Age of Enlightenment. Although known as an early champion of tolerance and freedom of thought, Voltaire did not show much tolerance toward Jews. In his writings he dismissed the Jewish religion as "detestable superstition" and went on to accuse the Jewish people of "sordid avarice" and "invincible hatred for every people by whom they are tolerated and enriched."[24]

The "sordid avarice" Voltaire refers to, drawn from the traditional hatred of the Jewish moneylender, fed the modern anti-Semitic stereotype of Jews as shrewd and scheming businessmen who were incapable of earning an honest living. Ironically, Voltaire made his own fortune as a moneylender. As Edouard Drumont wrote in a book called *Jewish France*:

> ....Jewish wealth...is essentially parasitical and usurious. It is not carefully husbanded fruit of the labor of innumerable generations. Rather, it is the result of speculation and fraud. It is not created by labor, but extracted with marvelous cleverness from the pocket of real workers by financial institutions, which have enriched their founders by ruining their stockholders....[25]

Drumont's book and others like it topped the best-seller lists in late nineteenth-century Europe.

Whole political parties in Europe were built on anti-Semitic platforms. During the 1890s, anti-Semitic parties entered the German parliament, and an avowed anti-Semite, Karl Lueger, was elected mayor of Vienna. In France, a national crisis exploded in 1897 over the unwarranted conviction for treason of Alfred Dreyfus, a Jewish army officer. While many Frenchmen acknowledged Dreyfus' innocence, anti-Semites saw in Dreyfus and his supporters a Jewish plot to defame and destroy the French military.

The Jews were placed in an awkward position. They were freer and more prosperous than ever before, and yet exposed to vicious political agitation. Threatened by this new kind of anti-Semitism, the Jews were not at all sure how best to confront it. Back in the days when the differences between Judaism and Christianity were purely religious, the Jews had a surefire response. They simply asserted the superiority of Judaism over Christianity or Islam and isolated themselves from an outside world which they considered corrupt. But the Jews were now *part* of the world at large, and the last thing they wanted to do was to keep themselves separated. What were they to do?

The answer formulated by Moritz Lazarus and many other Jewish leaders was that the fight against anti-Semitism was itself a patriotic act. It was a service to the fatherland. Anti-Semitism, Lazarus argued, is a form of intolerance and inhumanity that harms the entire nation, not only Jewish people. Because Jews were fully integrated into their homeland, it was their pride in Germany more than their Jewish spirit, that was hurt by anti-Semitic attacks.

Most Jews in the West believed that law, order and good sense would ultimately prevail. Some Jewish leaders therefore argued that the Jews should offer no public response at all to their enemies. One spokesman for French Jewry, encouraged by the support Dreyfus had received from much of French society, advised:

> We have only to await the indispensable protective measures and action on the part of the public authority: that is the reason why we rarely turn our attention to the systematic aggressions against our religion, and why we maintain an obligatory silence....[26]

Other Jewish leaders like Lazarus refused to remain silent. They felt it was time for the Jews to put their newly-won political and economic freedoms to good use. The Jews had to organize. They had to adopt the same tactics used by any other political or economic interest group that functions in a modern democracy. They must produce literature and lobby politicians for support. It is no coincidence that the great Jewish national and international organizations that exist today—such as the Anti-Defamation League of B'nai Brith and the Paris-based *Alliance Israelite Universelle*—originated as the response to modern anti-Semitism.

People like Lazarus were far more than politicians. They were idealistic Jews who believed that the best way to combat anti-Semitism was to increase an individual's pride in being Jewish. Lazarus was an active Reform Jew and firmly believed that Judaism represented the highest and purest form of monotheism. He, like many German Jews of his era, believed in a Jewish mission. As one German rabbi wrote:

> A higher duty has fallen to Israel in our time. You should not merely enjoy what the passage of time has brought you.....You must put to use that treasure which lies within you, carried through millennia and preserved throughout all times of suffering. You must use it now in its fully unleashed power for the benefit of the whole of society....From you has come the bubbling spring of the spirit, in order to pour it forth in a powerful stream over all educated mankind....[27]

In order to carry out their mission, Lazarus felt that the Jews must be models of ethical behavior. He was sharply critical of those Jews who did not live up to his high moral standards—so critical that one might say that he himself accepted some anti-Semitic beliefs as valid. Although Lazarus dismissed the baseless idea that Jews controlled world capitalism, he sincerely believed that Jews had an unhealthy tendency to pursue careers in business and finance. Such careers, he thought, were less morally elevating than academics or civil service, which directly served the fatherland. Ideally, he hoped, Jews would take up farming and handicrafts alongside their fellow Germans.

Some parts of Moritz Lazarus' program against anti-Semitism are still valid today. Others seem naive or misguided. But the program must be appreciated as the work of an idealistic and confident man who had the utmost faith in mankind's ability to overcome its darkest impulses. Lazarus did not understand that his noble efforts would prove futile, and that the anti-Semitic outrages of his time had unleashed a virulent destructive force in his beloved Germany.

STUDY QUESTIONS

1 During the Middle Ages, hatred of the Jews was sometimes called "anti-Judaism." In more recent times it has been called "anti-Semitism." Explain the difference between the two.

2 According to modern anti-Semites, what are considered typically Jewish "characteristics"? What connection do you see between these ideas and older forms of anti-Judaism?

3 Why does Lazarus consider anti-Semitism a problem for the whole nation and not just for the Jews? Why is the Jewish fight against anti-Semitism seen as a patriotic act?

4 Did all Jews rally around Lazarus' call to mount a public fight against anti-Semitism? What other responses does the chapter describe?

5 Looking at history through Lazarus' eyes, why do you think he was optimistic about the future of Jewish life in Germany?

6 The chapter explains that throughout Western Europe and North America the Jews were filled with patriotism for their homelands. Do you think the same was true in Eastern Europe? Why or why not?

7 Moritz Lazarus claimed that each people has a "special calling." What was the Jewish "calling" according to Lazarus and other Jews who share his view? How does this calling affect the way Jews combat anti-Semitism?

8 Jewish political organizations represented a new response to anti-Semitism. Why did such organizations arise during the nineteenth century? What did these organizations do to counteract anti-Semitism?

FOR DISCUSSION

A new form of anti-Semitism arose during the nationalistic period covered in this chapter. No longer considered solely as a religious group, Jews were despised as being an inferior race, a group of people who possessed physical and behavioral characteristics which were considered unattractive and damaging to the national character. What is the relationship between the rise of nationalism and this new form of anti-Semitism? How does this categorization of the Jews as a "race" differ from that of a "religious group?" Why is being labeled a "race" potentially more dangerous than being referred to as simply another religious sect?

As Russia expanded into new territories, it wanted to protect itself from the competition of Jewish merchants living in these areas. The Jewish merchants of Poland were forced to live in ghettos such as the one pictured here in Cracow. Contact, and therefore competition, between Russian merchants and Jewish merchants was thus eliminated.

THE PALE
OF SETTLEMENT

Anti-Semitism reached the level of mob violence and murder in Eastern Europe. Beginning in the year 1881, violent outbreaks spread throughout Roumania and the Russian Empire. These pogroms, and their underlying causes, deeply affected the attitudes of Russian Jews toward the non-Jewish world. The following selections are taken from the writings of Moshe Lieb Lilienblum and Peretz Smolenskin. The first was written by Lilienblum during a pogrom in his own village; the second was written by Smolenskin during a moment of calm after the storm.

May 5. Terrible! The situation is terrible and frightening! We are virtually under siege. The courtyards are barred up, and we keep peering through the grillwork of the court gates to see if the mob is coming down to swoop on us. All the furniture is stored in cellars, we all sleep in our clothes without any bedding... What does the future have in store for us? Will they have mercy on the youngsters—who don't even know yet that they are Jews, that they are wretches—and not harm them? Terrible, terrible! How long, O God of Israel?

May 7. I am glad I have suffered. The rioters approached the house I am staying in. The women shrieked and wailed, hugging the children to their breasts, and didn't know where to turn. The men stood by dumbfounded. We all imagined that in a few moments it would be all over with us....But, thank God, they were frightened away by the soldiers and we were not harmed. I am glad I have suffered. At least once in my life I have had the opportunity of feeling what my ancestors felt every day of their lives. Their lives were one long terror, so why should I experience nothing of the fright which they felt all their lives? I am their son, their sufferings are dear to me, and I am exalted by their glory....[28]

Calamity after calamity and disaster after disaster have afflicted the Jews of Russia. In many communities not a stone has been left standing. The shops of our brethren have been pillaged and looted, and whatever the mob could not carry off, it has utterly destroyed. Many

Jews have been murdered and the wounded are without number. The mob, a ravenous wolf in search of prey, has stalked the Jews with a cruelty unheard of since the Middle Ages. Perhaps most shocking of all, many supposedly decent people appeared among the makers of the pogroms. . . . At present our enemies in Russia are venting their rage by demanding that the Jews leave the country. This horrifies our brethren even more than all the disasters that have befallen us. But is it so wrong even for a Jew to say: Why should we not emigrate, if the government allows it? . . . . There is no doubt that it would be best for people who are leaving one country to migrate together to the same land, for they could then understand and help one another. If the wave of emigration is to direct itself to one place, surely no other country in the world is conceivable except Eretz Israel.[29]

Western European Jews in the nineteenth century looked confidently toward a bright future. They saw their homelands as bastions of liberty and freedom; anti-Semitism was considered a temporary irritant. The Jews of Eastern Europe found it far more difficult to justify such views. The bulk of European Jewry lived in the Russian Empire, the most backward of Europe's major states.

The Jews were crowded into an area of western Russia known as the Pale of Settlement. The Jews were not only forced to stay in the Pale, but even within its boundaries they were subject to periodic expulsions from their towns and villages. Jewish children lived under constant fear of army conscription, which carried a twenty-five year term and all but guaranteed that the child would be permanently severed from his family and his faith—even if he survived the term.

Anti-Semitism flourished among all segments of Russian society. Peasants and workers blamed Jewish peddlers and moneylenders for their poverty. The powerful Russian Orthodox Church ensured that the image of Jews as killers of Jesus Christ would not fade from the people's mind. The Jews were accused of both oppressing the poor and stealing from the rich. While the merchants saw Jews as competitors who must be squelched, Russian aristocrats looked down on the Jews as parasites that ought to be expelled from the nation. Referring to the millions of impoverished Jews in Russia, the Russian court counselor Pobedonostev stated: "A third will emigrate, a third will assimilate, and a third will die."

We saw in the last chapter that during the nineteenth century religious anti-Semitism gave way to political and racial anti-Semitism. This kind of anti-Semitism became particularly strong in Russia, where Russian officials were looking for scapegoats for the growing political and social unrest in the country. In the 1890s the Russian secret police produced a false document known as "The Protocols of the Elders of Zion" which accused the Jews of conspiring to take over the world.

[The leaders of international Jewry are assembled in a secret location. One of them says:] Whether the state is exhausted by inner turmoil, or whether through civil war it falls into the hands of external enemies, in either case it is doomed: it is in our power! The rule of capital, over which we alone have control, holds out a straw which the state must grasp, for good or ill, if it does not want to sink into the depths . . . . Our right lies in might . . . .Our motto is Power and Hypocrisy. . . .[W]e must not hesitate at bribery, fraud and treason when these can help us to reach our end. In politics it is necessary to seize the property of others without hesitation if in so doing we attain submission and power.[30]

Russian society was steeped in the belief that the Jew was the ultimate enemy. Pogroms and oppressive laws were the means by which the Jew was to be expelled from the nation. To some extent, Russian anti-Semitism had its desired effect: Between 1881 and 1914 some 2,000,000 Jews fled Russia. But the Jewish response was active as well as passive. It went beyond the genteel speechmaking encountered in the previous chapter. Throughout Russia Jews began to take up arms in self-defense against rampaging mobs. Jewish writers became quite bitter on those occasions when the Jews failed to defend themselves against attack, as shown by this scathing poem by Haim Nachman Bialik after a dreadful pogrom against the Jews of the town of Kishinev in 1903:

> Crushed in their shame, they saw it all;
> They did not stir nor move;
> They did not pluck their eyes out; they
> beat not their brains against the wall!
> Perhaps, perhaps, each watcher had it in his heart to pray;
> *A miracle, O Lord—and spare my skin this day!*
> Those who survived this foulness, who from their blood awoke,
> Beheld their life polluted, the light of their world gone out—
> How did their menfolk bear it, how did they bear this yolk?
> They crawled forth from their holes, they fled to the house of the Lord,
> They offered thanks to Him, the sweet benedictory word.
> The *Cohanim* sallied forth, to the Rabbi's house they flitted:
> *Tell me, O Rabbi, is my own wife permitted?*
> The matter ends; and nothing more.
> And all is as it was before . . . [31]

This poem provides an unusually savage example of a kind of self-criticism that Russian Jewish intellectuals had been leveling at their fellow Jews for decades. Before 1881 a school of Russian-Jewish intellectuals, called ''maskilim'' or ''the enlightened,'' had urged the Jews to adopt Russian culture in order to be accepted by Russian society. Two such intellectuals were Lilienblum and Smolenskin. But the pogroms forced these intellectuals to see that Russia would not accept its Jews on any terms, and that the Jews' effort to adopt gentile ways were destructive and humiliating. Smolenskin wrote:

> We have no sense of national honor; our standards are those of second-class people. We find ourselves rejoicing when we are granted a favor and exulting when we are tolerated and befriended. Jewish writers sing aloud for joy when a Jew happens to be honored . . . . Alas for such kindness and tolerance and alas for our writers, poets, and speakers who praise them. What is the real sadness of our estate? It is not the woes inflicted on us by our enemies but the wounds caused by our own brethren. If we really want to help the victims of the pogroms, we must first proclaim unceasingly that we ourselves are responsible for our own inner weakness. We must turn from the path of

disaster we once chose, for we can still be saved . . . .

During the 1880s and 1890s, increasing numbers of Russian Jews turned to Zionism as the solution to the perpetual crisis of Jewish life in Eastern Europe. A Jewish community in Eretz Israel would provide a haven for persecuted Jews; it would also be the center of a Jewish cultural and spiritual renaissance. Between 1881 and 1891 some 30,000 Jews left Europe for Palestine, and many more times that number joined clandestine Zionist groups in the Russian Empire. In 1897 the Austrian Jewish journalist Theodore Herzl founded the World Zionist Organization, thereby making Zionism an organized international movement. The anguished yearnings of Lilienblum and Smolenskin had taken the first steps toward fulfillment.

STUDY QUESTIONS

1 In the early part of this century, where was anti-Semitism most violent? Why?

2 Who wrote "The Protocols of the Elders of Zion"? What purpose was it supposed to serve?

3 Reread the Bialik poem in this chapter. Why is the poem hostile to the Jewish men of Kishinev? Do you think Bialik's attack is fair? Why or why not?

4 How did pogroms affect the Zionist movement?

5 Who were the "maskilim"? What did they advocate?

6 How was Zionism viewed as a solution to the crisis of Jewish life in Eastern Europe?

7 "Jews can gain acceptance in society by mimicking non-Jewish ways." What arguments can you present in favor of this statement? What arguments against?

FOR DISCUSSION

Compare Bialik's poem with the *piyuttim* of chapter three. How does Bialik mock the sentiment of the Jews whose only recourse in the face of violence is to pray: "A miracle, O Lord—and spare my skin this day!"? How has Bialik redefined the role that the Jews must play in shaping their destiny? How does that affect the relationship between the Jews and God as expressed in the *piyuttim*? What is the relationship between the rise of Zionism and Bialik's beliefs?

Yad va-Shem, established in Jerusalem in 1953, stands as a memorial museum and library for the six million Jews lost in the Holocaust.

THE HOLOCAUST
AND AFTER

The persecution of Eastern European Jewry at the turn of the twentieth century was a prelude to the Holocaust. Between the years 1939 and 1945 five to six million Jews—two thirds of the European Jewish population—were murdered. Entire communities were devoured by the German death camps Buchenwald, Sobibor, Treblinka and Auschwitz. European Jewish civilization, perhaps the most vibrant and creative in the history of the Diaspora, was nearly obliterated.

The Holocaust has scarred and traumatized the Jews as no other tragedy in history. It has left Jews feeling angry, bewildered, and lost. The Jewish mood is best described by the sad and gentle prose of Elie Wiesel, survivor of Auschwitz. The following essay was written by Wiesel to commemorate the *Yahrzeit* of his father, who died at Buchenwald.

Stretched out on a plank of wood amid the multitude of blood-covered corpses, fear frozen in his eyes, a mask of suffering on the bearded, stricken mask that was his face, my father gave back his soul at Buchenwald. A soul useless in that place, and one he seemed to want to give back. But, he gave it up, not to the God of his fathers, but rather to the imposter, cruel and insatiable, to the enemy God. They had killed his God, they had exchanged him for another. How, then, could I enter the sanctuary of the synagogue tomorrow and lose myself in the sacred repetition of the revival without lying to myself, without lying to him? How could I act or think like everyone else, pretend that the death of my father holds a meaning calling for grief and indignation? . . .

I once knew a deeply religious man [at Auschwitz] who, on the Day of Atonement, in despair, took heaven to task, crying out like a wounded beast, "What do You want from me, God? What have I done to You? I want to serve You and crown You ruler of the universe, but You prevent me. I want to sing of Your mercy, and You ridicule me. I want to place my faith in You, dedicate my thought to You, and You do not let me. Why? Why?"

I also knew a free-thinker, who one evening, after a selection, suddenly began to pray, sobbing like a whipped child. He beat his breast, became a martyr. He had need of support, and even more, of certitude; if he suffered, it was because he had sinned; if he endured torment, it was because he had deserved it.

Loss of faith for some equaled discovery of God for others. Both answered to the same need to take a stand, the same impulse to rebel. In both cases, it was an accusation. Perhaps some day someone will explain how, on the level of man, Auschwitz was possible; but on the level of God, it will forever remain the most disturbing of mysteries.

Many years have passed since I saw my father die. I have grown up and the candles I light several times a year in memory of departed members of my family have become more and more numerous. I should have acquired the habit, but I cannot. And each time the eighteenth day of the month of Shivat approaches, I am overcome by desolation and futility; I still do not know how to commemorate the death of my father, Shlomo ben Nissel, a death which took him as if by mistake.

Yes, a voice tells me that in reality it should suffice, as in previous years, to follow the trodden path: to study a chapter of *Mishna* and to say *Kaddish* once again, that beautiful and moving prayer dedicated to the departed, yet in which death itself figures not at all. Why not yield? It would be in keeping with the custom of countless generations of sages and orphans. By studying the sacred texts, we offer the dead continuity if not peace. It was thus that my father commemorated the death of his father.

But that would be too easy. The Holocaust defies reference, analogy. Between the death of my father and that of his, no comparison is possible. It would be inadequate, indeed unjust, to imitate my father. I should have to invent other prayers, other acts. And I am afraid of not being capable or worthy.

All things considered, I think that tomorrow I shall go to the synagogue after all. I will light the candles, I will say *Kaddish*, and it will be for me a further proof of my impotence.[32]

Elie Wiesel has a profound message that commands our attention. It is important to understand, however, that his is only one of several responses that Jews have formulated when confronted with the Holocaust. Wiesel is searching for the meaning of the Holocaust for Jews today; one must begin with how Jews responded to it while it was under way.

There are many misunderstandings and misperceptions about how European Jews confronted the Nazi threat. Some people argue bitterly that the Jews went to their deaths passively, "like sheep." Such arguments overlook the armed revolts launched by Jews against the Germans in the ghettos of Vilna, Warsaw, Bialystok and other cities. Most of the time the leaders of these ghetto uprisings were members of Zionist pioneer youth groups, which instilled into their members a great spiritual power. As Zivia Lubetkin, a survivor of the Warsaw ghetto rebellion, explained:

We were able to endure the life in the ghetto because we knew that we were a *collective*, a movement. Each of us knew that he wasn't alone. Every other Jew faced his fate alone, one man before the overpowering, invincible enemy. From the very first moment until the bitter end, we stood together, as a collective, a movement. The feeling that there was a movement, a community of people who cared about each other, who shared ideas and values in common, made it possible for each of us to do what we did. The greatest tragedy was that the Jews did not know what to do. From the very first days of demoralization in the ghetto until the final days of destruction and death, they did not know what to do. We knew. Our movement values showed us our goals and how to achieve them. This was the source of our strength to live. It is the very same source which keeps the survivors alive even today.[33]

As much as we revere the actions of Zivia Lubetkin and those like her, it would be unfair to the Holocaust victims to suggest that violent resistance was the only suitable Jewish response to Nazi occupation. Many Jews felt that it might be possible to survive the war by acquiescing to Nazi rule, not by launching a suicidal revolt against an insuperable enemy. Jews clung to their traditional beliefs, forged by centuries of persecution, that at least some would survive if the community banded together and provided for its members as best it could. Finally, and most importantly, the Jews of Europe did not know of the scope of the destruction process. They knew that Jews were being transported to the east, and that many were being killed, but the systematic gassing of millions was something that no sane mind could comprehend.

The same combinations of courage, confusion and incomprehension that plagued European Jewry also affected Jews elsewhere in the world. Zionist leaders in Palestine and the United States believed that their principal task was to strengthen the Jewish homeland to which Jewish refugees would come after the war. Attempts to rescue European Jews, many felt, were a strain on Zionist resources and of little value. After all, the American and British governments refused to bomb Hitler's death camps, to confront Hitler publicly with his crimes—or even to take in Jewish refugees.

Despite these overwhelming obstacles, Jewish groups in America, working through the War Refugee Board, did save some 200,000 European Jews from certain death. But the American Jewish community was not yet sufficiently united nor politically organized to have exerted more influence on American foreign policy. It is a question of some controversy today whether a united front of Zionists and other Jewish groups might have been able to push the American government into more serious and successful rescue operations.

Our concern is not, however, with what might have been, but rather with how Jews responded when confronted with the threat of total annihilation. Jews acted in different ways according to their convictions, but it is important to stress that they *acted* and did not passively accept their doom.

It is important to know how Jews behaved during the Holocaust, just as it is a painful but necessary duty to study how the genocide took place in the Nazi death camps. But understanding the how of things brings us no closer to fathoming their why. Jews seeking the ultimate causes of the Holocaust must leave the realm of history and human action altogether. Instead, they must turn to God and rephrase the eternal question of why God allows evil to flourish in the world which He created.

This question, which so many people have asked when confronted with the Holocaust, was put most poignantly by the Hebrew poet Bialik back at the turn of the century. We saw in the previous chapter that Bialik wrote a poem criticizing the men of Kishinev after the pogrom of 1903. Significantly, Bialik then wrote a *second* poem about the pogrom, one that demonstrates a very different kind of anger from that displayed in the first poem:

Heavens, beg mercy for me!

If there is a god within you and if the God has a path in you—
And I have not found it—
Then pray for me!
I—My heart is dead
And there is no longer prayer on my lips.
And the hand has already weakened and there is no longer
hope.
How long, until when? how long?

Hangman! Here's a neck—come and slaughter!
Behead me like a dog—you have the arm and the axe.
The whole earth is a scaffold to me.
And we—we are the few!
My blood is permitted—strike the skull and murder's blood will
spurt,
Blood of babies and greyheads on your shirt—
And it will never be blotted out, never.

And if Justice exists—let it appear at once!
But if Justice should appear after I am wiped out from under the
sky,
Let its throne be hurled down forever!
And let the heavens rot with eternal evil,
And you too, evil-doers, go forth in your violence—
Live by your bloodshed and be cleansed by it.

And cursed be he who says: Avenge!
Satan has not yet devised
A revenge such as this: the revenge for the blood of a little child.
Let the blood pierce the abyss!
Let the blood pierce into the depths of darkness.
And let it eat away in the dark and undermine there
All the rotting foundations of the earth.

There is a clear parallel between this poem and our passage from Elie Wiesel. Both texts deal with a theology of doubt, a debate with God that may be only a monologue. But at least for Bialik, there was some therapeutic power in his harangues against his fellow Jews and God himself. With his impassioned language, Bialik was cleansing himself of his anger and trying to lead the Jews toward a more active, realistic understanding of their fate. But where Bialik shouts, Wiesel whispers; where Bialik writes in flowing verse, Wiesel writes in spare prose. After all, as the philosopher Theodore Adorno has written, in the face of the Holocaust every poem is an obscenity.

In his essay, Wiesel writes that "scholars and philosophers" would best "withdraw without daring to enter into the heart of the matter." "Auschwitz, by definition, is beyond their vocabulary." Indeed, we are tempted to respond to the Holocaust only with silence. We wish to remember that past but search for meaning in the here and now.

That search for meaning causes us to learn one essential lesson from the Holocaust. As the theologian Eugene Borowitz has written, the Holocaust may not have destroyed man's faith in God so much as his unjustified confidence in himself.

One source of guidance and wisdom many Jews are discovering is traditional Judaism. Jewish tradition does not have answers for all of the questions of the twentieth century, nor can it solve the enigma of the Holocaust, but it affirms the triumph of life over death and good over evil. It ensures that the Jewish spirit did not perish at Auschwitz but will live on to help guide the Jewish people through the troubled age in which we live.

STUDY QUESTIONS

1 What problem does Elie Wiesel face each year as the "yahrzeit" of his father's death approaches?

2 Why does Wiesel say that by studying the sacred texts we offer the dead "continuity if not peace"?

3 Some feel that the "Kaddish," a prayer which affirms the greatness of God, is meaningless in the face of the events of the Holocaust. Why do they think so?

4 The world at large has criticized European Jewry for being passive and allowing themselves to be "led to the slaughter." What do you think motivated many European Jews to act in this way?

5 Locate the quotation from Zivia Lubetkin. Why, in her view, were she and her friends in the Warsaw Ghetto able to face the Nazis with such courage?

6 How is the Bialik poem in this chapter different from the one in Chapter 7? Who is the object of the poet's wrath?

7 Reread our source from Elie Wiesel. How, according to Jewish tradition, does one commemorate the death of a loved one? Why does Wiesel feel that the traditional ways no longer suffice?

8 According to Wiesel, what different responses could the Holocaust evoke from a believing Jew and an agnostic? What do these responses have in common?

FOR DISCUSSION

The Holocaust has been the traumatic experience in Jewish history not only because of its scope, but because it has forced people to reconcile the idea of evil in the world with the belief in a just God. To have survived the Holocaust and to be able to believe in an all-powerful and just God was something many people were unable to do. However, as the contemporary Jewish philosopher Emil Fackenheim argued, to give up one's belief in God and the Jewish religion would be giving a belated victory to Hitler. What philosophical responses can you offer to people who question their understanding of God and Judaism after the atrocities of the Holocaust?

Even in America, the most open of societies, anti-Semitism appeared in such crude forms as this 1930's political poster and the only slightly more subtle advertisement for summer homes on Cape Cod.

"AMERICA IS DIFFERENT"

During the early years of the twentieth century the number of Jews at America's best private universities steadily increased. Harvard University's undergraduate enrollment, 6% Jewish in 1908, was 20% Jewish by 1920. Columbia University's was 40%. The administrators of Harvard feared that the school's gentlemanly Protestant image was being destroyed by the intrusion of a "foreign" element. They therefore imposed admission quotas to keep the number of Jews at Harvard down to a "reasonable" level. Harvard's decision brought about a famous exchange of letters in June, 1922, between the President of Harvard, A.L. Lowell, and a Jewish Harvard graduate, Alfred A. Benesch. The letters were published and became part of a Jewish fight against anti-Semitism in this country.

> My Dear Mr. Lowell: . . . .It is utterly impossible for me to comprehend how an institution of learning which has throughout its history received contributions from men of all religious faiths, and which has enjoyed an enviable reputation for non-sectarianism, can even contemplate the adoption of a regulation obviously designed to discriminate against the Jews . . . .Students of the Jewish faith neither demand nor expect any favors at the hands of the university; but they do expect, and have a right to demand, that they be admitted upon equal terms with students of other faiths, and that scholarship and character be the only standards of admission . . . .Very truly yours, Alfred A. Benesch

> Dear Mr. Benesch: . . . .[T]here is perhaps no body of men in the United States, mostly Gentiles, with so little anti-Semitic feelings as the instructing staff at Harvard University. But the problem that confronts this country and its educational institutions is a difficult one . . . .There is, most unfortunately, a rapidly growing anti-Semitic feeling in this country, causing—and no doubt in part caused by—a strong race feeling on the part of the Jews themselves . . . .The anti-Semitic feeling among the [college] students is increasing, and it grows in proportion to the increase in the number of Jews. If their number should become 40% of the student body, the race feeling would become in-

tense. When, on the other hand, the number of Jews was small, the race antagonism was small also. Any such race feeling among the students tends to prevent the personal intimacies on which we must rely to soften anti-Semitic feeling. If every college in the country would take a limited proportion of Jews, I suspect we should go along toward eliminating race feeling among the students, and as these students passed out into the world, eliminating it in the community....Respectfully yours, A.A. Lowell

Dear Mr. Lowell:....Although I agree with you that, unhappily, there is a rapidly growing anti-Semitic feeling in this country, I must take issue with you upon the proposition that this feeling is caused in part by a strong race feeling on the part of the Jews. Is not the strong race feeling on the part of the Jews the result rather than the cause? In other words, has not the strong race feeling been developed as a measure of self-defense?... Carrying your suggestion [about limiting Jewish enrollments] to its logical conclusion would inevitably mean that a complete prohibition against Jewish students in the colleges would solve the problem of anti-Semitism. Moreover, it might lead to the establishment of a distinctively Jewish university, a consummation most sincerely to be deplored. If it be true—and I have no doubt that it is true—that the anti-Semitic feeling among the students is increasing, should it not be the function of an institution of learning to discourage rather than to encourage such a spirit? If certain members of the student body foster so un-American a spirit, Harvard University, which has always stood for true democracy and liberalism, should be the first to condemn such a spirit, and exert every effort to prevent its growth....Respectfully yours, Alfred A. Benesch.[34]

The twentieth century has witnessed the ruination of European Jewry, but has also seen the prosperity of American Jewry. Jews have struck deep and solid roots in American soil; they have become an integral part of American society. This does not mean that anti-Semitism has been a stranger in America; far from it. But American society has been better able to resist the anti-Semitic virus and American Jews have been in a better position to fight anti-Semitic attacks.

Anti-Jewish feeling was part of the baggage brought by the first settlers into the New World. In 1654 the governor of New Amsterdam, Peter Stuyvesant, tried to prevent Jews from settling in the colony. William Penn forbade public Jewish worship in his colony of Pennsylvania. But in the mid-eighteenth century the ideals of the founding fathers of the United States—the ideals of equality and liberty discussed in chapter six—became central to American political life. The Jews, like all other citizens of the young republic, were guaranteed religious freedom.

Jews immigrating to this country in the mid-nineteenth century encountered a land of endless frontiers and economic opportunity. They also encountered sterotypes that had haunted them in Europe for centuries. During the decades before the Civil War, newspapers and novels frequently depicted Jews as greedy moneylenders. An article in a prominent New York newspaper described Judaism as a body of ''terrible opinions and doctrines'' aimed at the erosion of "all religion under the secret poison of infidelity and atheism."[35] And yet, despite these anti-Semitic slurs, Jews did not experience the riots and other persecutions they had known in Europe. In the city and on the frontier, Jews and non-Jews formed close social ties. American society seemed to have two contradictory images of the Jews, one a sort of fairy-tale demon, the other a real person, a neighbor.

The real test of American openness toward Jews came in the late nineteenth century, the so-called "gilded age" of American industrialization and urban growth. Americans confused by the lightning-fast changes in their society could not resist using the Jews as scapegoats. As in Europe, the Jew became the symbol of modern life, of the metropolis and its strange new ways. Beginning in the 1870s, Jews found themselves excluded from hotels, country clubs, resorts and neighborhoods. Banks and public utilities would not hire them. The ideas of Edouard Drumont and Richard Wagner found expression in books written on this side of the Atlantic, and the Jews were again categorized as a race.

Perhaps the worst excesses of American anti-Semitism came during the 1920s. Prior decades of waves of immigration from Europe—of which the Jews were only a part—had produced a hysterical xenophobia in many Americans. In the 1920s the automobile magnate Henry Ford published a thinly disguised version of the "Protocols of the Elders of Zion" in the Michigan newspapers he owned, the *Dearborn Independent*. This kind of popular anti-Semitism left its mark on the Jews. Jews were closed out of careers in major corporations, banks, engineering and law firms, and medicine. "The conventional wisdom of the time," one historian writes, "was that nine out of ten jobs in the white-collar occupations in the major cities were closed to Jewish applicants."[36] And as we saw from our main text, the gates of Ivy League colleges were closed to all but a small percentage of Jews.

American anti-Semitism in this century has been real and dangerous. Only after World War II did the American business and professional world open up to Jews; many doors still remain closed. But there are inner strengths in American society and in its Jewish community that have helped push anti-Semitism out of mainstream thought to the fringes. First, Jews were quick to form organizations such as the American Jewish Committee, founded in 1906, and the Anti-Defamation League of B'nai Brith, which since 1913 has combatted anti-Semitic libels in the press, plays and films. Even more so than in Western Europe, Jews in America were willing to take on anti-Semites in direct battles. Political lobbying, information campaigns, economic boycotts and court suits have all been part of the American Jewish arsenal in the fight against anti-Semitism.

Our text shows how an American Jew did not fear to launch a public campaign against one of this country's most powerful institutions. Although Benesch's letters could not shake the stubborn and snobbish Lowell, other Jewish battles were more successful. For example, the ADL protested the way Hollywood filmmakers portrayed Jews. Before the ADL was formed, Jews were routinely depicted in films "in a manner similar to that employed on the burlesque and vaudeville stages....Under the guise of fun, the most sordid, vulgar and unclear characteristics were frequently attributed to Jews in general."[37] By the 1920s these stereotypes were off the screen.

American Jews fighting anti-Semitism have had a great advantage over Jews elsewhere—the American political system tends to favor the Jewish cause. Our republic is and has been committed to religious freedom and the separation of church and state. Even when anti-Semitism was at its height,

Jews found supporters among America's most powerful and respected leaders. For example, in 1921, 119 prominent Christians, including President Woodrow Wilson and ex-President William H. Taft, signed a declaration that stated:

> We believe it should not be left to men and women of Jewish faith to fight this evil, but that it is in a very special sense the duty of citizens who are not Jews by ancestry or faith. We therefore make earnest protest against this vicious propaganda, and call upon our fellow citizens of Gentile birth and Christian faith to unite their efforts to ours, to the end that it may be crushed....[38]

There is one final reason why anti-Semitism in America has been less fierce than in Europe, and it has little to do with American democracy or Jewish activism. The fact is that the United States has always been home to a much broader mix of ethnic and racial groups than Europe. America is a melting pot, a nation of immigrants.

American Jews have often looked at the tragic history of European Jewry and said with relief, "America is different." Indeed, America *is* different. Jewish life has flourished in the United States in ways that even the most privileged European Jews could not have imagined. Anti-Semitism has for the most part been kept at bay. American Jews have controlled anti-Semitism partly by using the political and economic freedoms that are the pillars of the American republic. But in the end, it is the openness of American society that has produced the most hospitable environment for Jews in the history of their dispersion.

STUDY QUESTIONS

1 What is "xenophobia"? How are Jews affected by it?

2 "Affirmative action," which requires a minimum number of minorities to fill certain positions, is one modern remedy for the evils of discriminatory quotas. What do you think of this method as a tool against discrimination in general and anti-Semitism in particular?

3 What do you think the reaction of Mr. Benesch would have been to the establishment in 1948 of Brandeis University, a nonsectarian yet Jewish-sponsored institution?

4 What are "the inner strengths in American society and in its Jewish community" which have helped overcome and prevent mainstream anti-Semitism?

5 In Mr. Lowell's response to Mr. Benesch, how does he say he can "eliminate race feeling" among the students at Harvard? What is your reaction to his solution?

6 What contribution did Presidents Taft and Wilson make to combat anti-Semitism?

FOR DISCUSSION:

The Anti-Defamation League influenced the way in which Jews were characterized by Hollywood. They successfully pressured the moviemakers to avoid stereotyping Jews in a derogatory way. Shylock, a character from Shakespeare's *Merchant of Venice*, is often viewed as an anti-Semitic portrait of a stereotypically greedy Jewish moneylender. Some theater groups and audience have, therefore, shunned performances of this classic play. What is your reaction?

NOTES

CHURCH VERSUS SYNAGOGUE

1 Chrysostom, cited in James Parkes, *The Conflict of the Church and the Synagogue: A Study in the Origins of Antisemitism* (New York: Atheneum, 1981), 164.

THE CRUSADES

2 Translated by Jacob Marcus, *The Jew in The Modern World* (New York: Atheneum, 1938), 115-121.
3 Cited in Leon Poliakov, *The History of Anti-Semitism, Vol. 1: From the Time of Christ to the Court Jews* (New York: Vanguard, 1974), 30-31.
4 Abraham Haberman, ed., *Sefer G'zerot be-Ashkenaz u-Tsarfat*, 1945, 24.
5 Poems translated by T. Carmi, *The Penguin Book of Hebrew Verse* (New York: Penguin Books, 1981), 374-5, 376, 377-9.

TRIAL AND EXILE

6 Translated by Hyam Maccoby, *Judaism on Trial: Jewish-Christian Disputations in the Middle Ages* (New York: Oxford University Press, 1982), 117-147.
7 Cited in Solomon Grayzel, *The Church and the Jews in the XIII Century*, 1966, 241.
8 Cited in H.H. Ben-Sasson, *A History of the Jewish People* (New York: Harvard University Press, 1976), 708.
9 Translated by T. Carmi, *op. cit.*, 347-349.

DAR AL-ISLAM

10 The word "madman" (meshuga) is used in the Bible to describe false prophets; see Jeremiah 29:26.
11 Translated by Norman Stillman, *The Jews of Arab Lands* (Philadelphia: Jewish Publication Society, 1979), 233-246.
12 Translated by Stillman, *op. cit.*, 157.
13 Ibn Kammuma, *Examination of Three Faiths*, translated by Moshe Perlmann (Berkley and Los Angeles: The University of California Press, 1971), 149.
14 Translated by T. Carmi, *op.cit.*, 324.
15 Bernard Lewis, *The Jews of Islam* (Oxford: Oxford University Press, 1985), 170.
16 Alexander Russel, *The Natural History of Aleppo*, 2d ed., Vol. II (Westmead, England: Gregg International, 1969 reprint), reproduced in Stillman, *op. cit.*, 319.
17 Edward William Lane, *The Manners and Customs of the Modern Egyptians* (London: Darf Publishers Ltd., 1978 reprint), reproduced in Stillman, *op. cit.*, 327.

EMANCIPATION

18 A German anti-Semitic preacher and politician.
19 A reference to the famous anti-Semitic statement, "The Jews are our misfortune!" made in 1879 by the German historian Heinrich von Treitschke.
20 Moritz Lazarus, *Unser Standpunkt. Zwei Reden an seine Religionsgenossen am 1. und 16 December 1880*, Berlin, 1881, 3-15.
21 Cited in Michael Marrus, *The Politics of Assimilation* (New York: Oxford University Press, 1971), 94.
22 Cited in Paul Mendes-Flohr and Jehuda Reinharz, eds., *The Jew in the Modern World* (New York: Oxford University Press, 1980), 273.
23 Translated by W.A. Ellis, "Judaism in Music," *Richard Wagner's Prose Works* (New York: Scholarly, 1894), 82-3. Cited in Paul Mendes-Flohr and Jehuda Reinharz, eds., *The Jew in the Modern World, op. cit.*
24 Translated by W.F. Fleming, "Jews," *The Works of Voltaire: The Philosophical Dictionary*, (New York: Gordon Press, 1901), 284.
25 Edouard Drumont, *La France Juive*, 115th ed., Paris, 527. Cited in Mendes-Flohr and Reinharz, eds., *The Jew in the Modern World, op. cit.*
26 Cited in Marrus, *op. cit.*, 143.
27 From a sermon by the celebrated leader of German Liberal Judaism, Abraham Geiger, in his *Nachgelassene Schriften*, Ludwig Geiger, ed., Vol. V, Berlin, 1875-1878, I, 431.

THE PALE OF SETTLEMENT

28 Moshe Lieb Lilenblum, "The Way of Return," *The Zionist Idea*, Arthur Hertzberg ed. (New York: Temple Books, 1959).
29 Peretz Smolenskin, "Let Us Search Our Ways," *ibid.* 148-151.
30 *Die Geheimnisse der Weisen von Zion*, Gottfried zur Beek ed., 17th ed., Verlag Frz. Eher Nachf., Munich, 1933, 22-25.
31 Translated by Abraham M. Klein, *The Complete Works of H.N. Bialik*, ed. Israel Efros (New York: Bloch Publishing, 1948), 133-134.

THE HOLOCAUST AND AFTER

32 Elie Wiesel, *Legends of Our Time* (New York: Henry Holt, 1968), 15-16, 19-21.
33 Zivia Lubetkin, *In the Days of Destruction and Revolt* (Tel Aviv: Ha-Kibbutz Ha Meuhad/Am Oved, 1981), 277-278.

34 Reproduced in Marc Lee Raphael, *Jews and Judaism in the United States: A Documentary History* (New York: Behrman House, 1983), 292-297.
35 *New York Herald,* November 18, 1837, cited in Jonathan Sarna, "American Anti-Semitism," *History and Hate: The Dimensions of Anti-Semitism,* ed. David Berger, (Philadelphia: Jewish Publication Society, 1986), 119.
36 Nathan Belth, *A Promise to Keep: A Narrative of the American Encounter with Anti-Semitism* (New York: Schocken, 1979), 112-113.
37 *Report of the Anti-Defamation League,* May, 1915, reproduced in Yehuda Reinharz and Paul Mendes-Flohr, eds., *The Jew in the Modern World* (New York: Oxford University Press, 1980), 404.
38 *The New York Times,* January 16, 1921, 31, reproduced in Reinharz and Mendes-Flohr, *op. cit.,* 409-410.

PHOTO CREDITS

American Jewish Historical Society 58 / Bibliothèque Nationale, Paris 4, 18, 38 / Rosegarten Museum 24 / Victor Laredo 32 / Vishniac 46 / Yad va-Shem, Jerusalem 52